READ & WRITE IT OUT LOUD!

Guided Oral Literacy Strategies

KEITH POLETTE

The University of Texas at El Paso

PEARSON

Boston   New York   San Francisco
Mexico City   Montreal   Toronto   London   Madrid   Munich   Paris
Hong Kong   Singapore   Tokyo   Cape Town   Sydney

Senior Series Editor: *Aurora Martínez Ramos*
Editorial Assistant: *Erin Beatty*
Marketing Manager: *Jennifer Armstrong*
Manufacturing Buyer: *Andrew Turso*
Cover Designer: *Kristina Mose-Libon*
Production Editor: *Won Jang*
Composition and Prepress Buyer: *Linda Cox*
Electronic Composition: *Cabot Computer Services*

Library of Congress Cataloging-in-Publication Data

Polette, Keith.
    Read & write it out loud! : guided oral literacy strategies / Keith Polette.
      p.   cm.
    Includes bibliographic references and index.
    ISBN 0-205-40565-7 (pbk.)
      1. Oral reading. 2. Language arts (Elementary). 3. Language arts (Middle school).
    I. Title: Read and write it out loud! II. Title.

LB1573.5.P65   2005
372.45'2—dc22

                              2004044325

MAR 0 1 2006

CONTENTS

CHAPTER 4

Teaching Children to Read Aloud: Strategies That Develop Expressive and Interpretative Reading Skills   40

CHAPTER 5

Writing to Read Aloud: Reasons and Ways to Write for the Expressive Voice   52

CHAPTER 6

Ready to Read Aloud Scripts: Poetry, Prose, and Drama   105

REFLECTIONS ON READING

*The basic model of reading is silent . . . yet making
sense is the same in oral and silent reading.*
—Yetta M. Goodman and Kenneth S. Goodman,"To Err Is Human:
Learning about Language Processes by Analyzing Miscues"

*We have to demonstrate that reading is as much fun as talking, and almost as
necessary. We have to create in children a deep* need *for books.*
—Mem Fox, *Radical Reflections*

*[I]f the goal of reading instruction is to help children interact meaningfully
with a variety of texts, they must be competent in word recognition, read
at a suitable rate, and understand how to project the phrasing and
expression of the spoken word upon the written word.*
—Meribethe Richards, "Be a Good Detective: Solve the Case of Oral Reading Fluency"

*We know that speaking, reading, and writing help us discover not merely what
we want or think or say or do—but also what we want to* become.
—Roy F. Fox, "Beating the Moon: A Reflection on Media and Literacy"

When we think of "reading," we usually think of *silent* reading, and we conjure images of solitary, happy, noiseless readers clutching books, magazines, or newspapers. We imagine these readers absorbed in their reading, their eyes running across lines of print from left to right and back again, while their minds make marvelous meaning from the words that dance and cavort through them.

When we think of "reading," however, we usually do not think of *oral* reading—of happy, noisy, audience-surrounded readers delivering voice-fulls of print. The standard image of reading is not one where we imagine readers standing before crowds of rapt listeners who hang on the readers' words, responding with awes or sobs, applauding spoken prose or poetry because it was expressed with powerful emotion, perfect pitch, and pleasing intonation.

Moreover, when we listen to most children—and many adults—read aloud, we do not hear the strains of language rendered in wondrous audio shapes that satiate the ear, vivify the heart, or enliven the mind. Rather, we often hear words in distress—words unhappily pulled from the page and spoken in tones that dull the ear, blanch the heart, and bore the mind.

Words read aloud by many children are in distress because most of these oral readers are stressed when reading. Often nervous and unsure, they read either too fast or too slow, too soft or too loud, too monotonously or too haltingly. Whatever the case, oral reading is something we often don't want to hear because it does not engage us. And so, in many cases, oral reading has become the infrequent sideshow of reading, the lost sheep of literacy—something heard or done on rare occasions.

But why has oral reading been sent so often to the fringes of human activity? Why does it so frequently occupy the forgotten outpost of what we do with printed words?

First, few people seem to know how to read aloud well. Most of us are not trained to read aloud expressively, nor are we surrounded by models of proficient, fluent, lively oral reading. Without access to training or exposure to models, it is no wonder that few people read aloud well. And since few people seem to know how to do it, most children will not learn it. We can only teach what we know. If we don't know how to read aloud well, we won't be able to teach children how to do it successfully.

One problem is that few adults—apart from some teachers and parents—read aloud anymore. Gone are the days when poets, scops, and storytellers roamed the land and recited rich texts to eager audiences. Gone are the days when children and adults alike sat enraptured for hours and became entwined by the weave of language that was spun into their ears. No longer a priority, the art and practice of expressive oral reading has nearly faded into obscurity. As this art has almost faded, so too has the modeling of expressive language—modeling that children need. Many children no longer have powerful readers to emulate.

Now, in place of the lively and fully embodied human voice, is the electronic media. On TV, for instance, one will almost never hear hours of rich language read well by someone proficient at reading. Rather, TV generally presents its audience with simplified language—language stripped of poetic essence, language diminished into small words and short sentences, language that is the weak stepchild of a wide range of fast-driven images. TV language is most often the language of the sound bite, of cute quips, of shallow exchanges, and of canned commodities; it rarely contains the stuff that stimulates the imagination, sharpens the mind, or fires the heart. It should not surprise us to learn, then, that most TV language is geared to somewhere between the fourth- and sixth-grade level of usage. To be blunt: the language of most TV programs descends to the lowest level; it is designed never to challenge viewers, never to make them feel unintelligent, but always to keep them viewing, not thinking or speaking or reading (Scheuer 1999).

Children, though, are hungry for words (Healy 1987). Their brains are like sponges constantly ready to soak up new words and phrases. But if their primary access to language is via TV, then that is the only kind of language they will know and internalize—and that is the only kind of language they will be able to read, write, speak, and think.

Second, it may seem a difficult task to evaluate—to grade—how well children read aloud. Most of us know a good oral reader when we hear one, but do we know precisely what makes the reader good? Do we know, specifically, why one reader is better than another? And, more importantly, can we devise a fair and equitable way of evaluating each? Because we may not have deduced those specific criteria that are involved in effective oral reading, we have not devised methods of evaluation—methods that are fair and not entirely subjective.

Third, with the nationwide emphasis on silent standardized testing, oral reading gets even shorter shrift. Standardized testing purports to be objective and reliable in its ability to measure children's capacities to demonstrate how well they can use discreet reading skills. Whether this is true is debatable. But one thing is sure: a silent, fill-in-the-blanks, standardized test cannot measure a child's capacity to read aloud well. And since oral reading ability cannot be measured by a standardized test, it is not central in most curricula.

One important thing that has been lost with the marginalization of oral reading is an exciting and powerful means for helping children learn to love, understand, internalize, and use language that may not otherwise be readily available to them. When it is taught effectively, oral reading—being akin to how children learn and use language naturally—can help children discover a passion for reading, develop a wide range of essential reading skills, and assist them in developing confidence in themselves as readers.

This book is designed to help both adults and children rediscover the power, potency, and pleasure of oral reading. Chapter 1 discusses why adults need to read aloud to children. Chapter 2 discusses the dynamic benefits of teaching children to read aloud; it also includes a discussion of the skills that children need to learn to become effective, excited, and successful oral readers. Chapter 3 offers strategies for reading aloud to children; each strategy helps children develop active and critical listening skills. Chapter 4 contains guided strategies to help children become successful oral readers. Chapter 5 explains why children need to create their own read-aloud texts; it includes explicit writing activities that lead to the creation of read-aloud vehicles. Chapter 6 contains texts that are ready to be read aloud by both adults and children: poetry, prose, and drama.

By presenting ideas and strategies for reciting, reading, writing, and listening, this book envisions and explains literacy as an integrated process. Since language is not static but dynamic, our approach to using and understanding it must also be dynamic. As such, we need to help children learn how to recite, read, write, and listen in ways that help them discover the vibrancy of language.

The ideas, strategies, techniques, activities, and scripts in this book are structured to be used when and how they are needed. They are also designed so that both adults and children can come to know the great joys and many benefits of reading aloud—benefits that can result in the development of a deep and enduing *need* to bring books and self-authored texts to life via the vigorous, expressive voice.

ACKNOWLEDGMENTS

Many thanks to the following reviewers for their time and input: Deb Carr, King's College and Hazleton Area School District; Michael Moore, Georgia Southern University; and Judith O'Laughlin, New Jersey City University.

CHAPTER ONE

READING ALOUD TO CHILDREN

Reasons and Resources

*Our understanding of literacy must begin with the recognition
of orality and its continuing presence in our lives.*
—Margaret Meek, *On Being Literate*

*For skillful reading, the connections between print
and language must be thoroughly developed.*
—Marilyn Jager Adams, *Beginning to Read: Thinking and Learning about Print*

*The verbal interaction between adult and child that occurs during
story readings has a major influence on children's literacy.*
—Carol Vukelich, James Christie, and Billie Enz, *Helping
Young Children Learn Language and Literacy*

*Reading aloud to children builds knowledge about the world beyond the daily
environment; expands vocabulary and understanding; stimulates imagination;
fosters emotional growth; and is an advertisement for the pleasures of reading.*
—Marian Diamond and Janet Hopson, *Magic Trees of the Mind*

The history of literature shares a unique feature with how children learn language: they both are fixed in spoken speech (Meek 1991; McCracken & McCracken 1986; Ong 1982). For thousands of years before the radical transformations brought about by the industrial revolution of the nineteenth century and the electronic revolution of the twentieth century, literature was primarily experienced as an oral activity.

Before most people had access to books or were able to read, they listened to literature read aloud or performed. For these listeners, literature was a lively drama, a dynamic and immediate experience that communicated ideas, emotions, and images on cognitive, imaginative, and emotional levels simultaneously. Literature, as it was read aloud, also formed the basis of a communal activity, one that brought people together, allowed them to share a power-ful word-borne experience, and enabled them to construct meaning socially.

Just as literature had its beginnings in orality, so too do children (Ratey 2002). Prior to being able to read, they swim in a sea of words that they have heard but cannot decipher from the printed page. In this wordy sea, they actively gather language and build vocabularies through the ear—through the words they hear (Fox 1993). For them, language is a dynamic, verbal and audio experience; it has not yet become an abstraction—that is, it is not yet a series of linguistic structures to be studied silently in books. Rather, language is a potent and mysteri-ous presence, one that exerts a strong shaping power on their minds and perceptions (Csikszentmihalyi 1991).

With many schools in most states placing emphasis on activities and tests that are based on silent reading, the power of the oral tradition of literature, and the way that children natu-rally acquire language, is fading and may disappear. One of the most important things that has been lost is the experience of the communal and procreative nature of language—the role of language in creating and sustaining a community of engaged people who construct meaning by actively listening and responding to literature read expressively.

When oral literature loses its place in the communal lives of children (and adults!), language itself becomes diminished and thought becomes simplistic—something that Ralph Waldo Emerson stated over one hundred years ago and that George Orwell and Archibald MacLeish reminded us of nearly half a century ago. While silent reading must indeed be an important part of children's ongoing literacy development, an exclusive emphasis on it will not provide fully realized access to the communal and constructive power of language and literature.

To re-inaugurate the oral tradition of literature, we must retrieve oral language from the fringes of our lives and from the forgotten places in our schools and make it a central part of how we help children develop literacy and a love of literature. This means two things: first, we must read aloud to children every day, and second, we must teach children how to read aloud expressively.

A MODEL OF READING

While there are many models and theories that attempt to define reading, it is probably safe to say that most theorists would agree that reading is a multilevel process in which readers use their prior knowledge and previous experiences to construct meaning, actively and purpose-fully, based on their interaction with the printed page. As such, readers construct meaning by employing both cognition (the ability to predict, reason, infer, and draw conclusions) and imagination (the ability to form mental images, make aesthetic associations, and establish empathetic responses). If we also employ ideas from Rumelhart's model (1994), we can ex-pand our own definition of reading to see that it includes six important cueing systems that successful readers use:

> *Graphophonic cues:* sound-letter correspondences (phonics); readers use grapho-phonic cues to sound out and decode words
>
> *Lexical cues:* word recognition (but not necessarily word meaning); readers use lexi-cal cues to recognize words and word units

Syntactic cues: structural correspondence; readers use syntactic cues to make sure what they are reading "sounds right" and is organized in a way that makes sense

Semantic cues: word-meaning correspondences; readers use semantic cues to read connotatively, to understand concepts, to draw inferences, and to recognize subtle differences between words

Schematic cues: prior knowledge/previous experience correspondences; readers use schematic cues (i.e., what they already know and the language they have already internalized) as a basis for making sense of, and drawing conclusions about, what they are reading

Pragmatic cues: purpose/intention correspondences; readers use pragmatic cues to establish purposes for reading, methods of constructing meaning, and interacting with others in a social environment to create more sophisticated and conceptual interpretations of what they have read

Effective readers use all six cueing systems and create multiple levels of meaning from what they read. Struggling readers do not use all six cueing systems; they may understand a part of what they are reading, but they will miss the whole. Moreover, when readers attend only to the denotative aspect of what they are reading (decoding), they are doing little more than calling out words and are not constructing deep meaning.

To be successful, readers must use all six cueing systems and they must set their own purposes for reading (to enjoy, to gather information, to evaluate, etc.); they must examine the text prior to reading and set their expectations as to the kind of text it is and what their experience with it might be; they must choose a method of reading (preview and read, skim/scan and read, read from beginning to end, read only selected parts, read and reread, etc.); and readers must decide how to respond to what they have read (mental summary, evaluation of the text, an emotional response, etc.) (Almasi 2003; Au, Carroll, & Scheu 2001; Smith 1997).

REASONS TO READ ALOUD TO CHILDREN

If we want to help children learn to use cognition, imagination, and all six cues when they read, we need to get them excited about reading through energetic guidance and proactive practice. One of the most effective ways to guide children into becoming stronger readers and to give them the necessary mental practice for doing so is to read aloud to them every day. There is no substitute for regularly reading aloud to children; when we do so, we are helping them create meaning the way they do naturally—via the ear (Sanders 1995). Here are ten essential reasons for reading aloud:

1. *To provide enjoyment.* Children generally love being read to by someone who enjoys reading aloud. In such a situation, children discover how much fun it is to listen to literature and how powerful literature is in stimulating their imaginations (Egan 1992). When they are read to, children are transported into new worlds—ones that they create in their own minds, ones born of words, and ones charged with emotive energy. Only by listening to literature can children initially learn how to create fully embodied worlds in their minds. Because children will not become good at something they don't enjoy doing, we must offer them literature-based experiences that are positive, engaging, and enjoyable. When children come to see and experience literature as something fun, as something positive, as something that leads them beyond themselves, then they will be much more willing and interested in learning how to become readers themselves (McKean 2001).

2. *To model expressive reading.* Since most children have little exposure to models of effective, expressive reading, we need to fill that gap. For the majority of children, the only models of reading that they hear are media-driven: television programming and advertising, movie-talk, and radio-speech. And, for the most part, the media does not deliver rich language that is read by someone skilled in the art of reading aloud (Scheuer 1999; Singer & Singer 1990). Just as children try to imitate the antics of a favorite musician, athlete, or actor/actress, so too will they want to imitate someone who is a passionate and powerful oral reader (McKean 2001; Richards 2000). More importantly, by listening to models of expressive reading, children will learn that there is great art and skill (and magic!) involved in being able to transform the immobile ink marks on the page into a powerful performance and an enriching experience (Martinez, Roser, & Strecker 1999; Johns & VanLeirsburg 1994).

3. *To show the connections between speech and print.* When children hear literature read aloud, they see how printed words can be closely connected with spoken words. Because the organization and arrangement of most printed texts are different from the organization and arrangement of most spoken language (Ong 1982), children need to be shown how to make bridges of understanding between these two worlds. Often children try to apply the unspoken rules of spoken speech (spoken ideas are often fragmented, not fully developed, not formally organized, and not connected to a central idea) to print language and are unsuccessful (Dunn 2001). When they hear literature read aloud, however, they begin to make the important links between the speech they have internalized and the speech they are hearing (Harvey & Goudvis 2000; Popp 1996).

4. *To help children develop stronger vocabularies and more sophisticated language structures.* Since children acquire language primarily through the ear, the words they hear are

■ ■ ■ ■ ■ ▬▬▬▬▬▬▬▬▬▬▬▬▬▬▬▬▬▬▬▬▬▬▬▬▬▬▬▬▬▬▬▬▬▬

REASONS TO READ ALOUD TO CHILDREN

1. To provide enjoyment.
2. To model expressive reading.
3. To show the connections between speech and print.
4. To help children develop stronger vocabularies and more sophisticated language structures.
5. To introduce different genres and writing styles.
6. To increase attention span.
7. To strengthen cognitive ability.
8. To enhance the affective domain.
9. To help second language learners become familiar with the sounds and shapes of English.
10. To meet national literacy standards.

central to their ability to understand and use words in speech and create meaning from words in print. If children don't regularly hear new words in new contexts, they will not be able to add them to their mental storehouse of words. Moreover, children will be limited in their abilities to read and write based on the number of words and language structures they have in their minds (Orr 2000). The fewer words that children have internalized, the more limited will be their ability to read (Smith 1997). If children haven't internalized words and sentence patterns, they will not be able to read or write them (Healy 1990). If children are to become successful, independent readers, they will need to have a large, active, mental storehouse of words and language structures (sentences, paragraphs, poems, stories, etc.). When they are regularly exposed to words and language patterns that are outside their normal way of speaking, children develop a stronger awareness of language and its aesthetic and communicative possibilities. Entwined with this stronger awareness is a natural desire to put to use these new words and patterns. This new linguistic awareness will make itself known in the way children speak and write—and in their ability to read and understand increasingly sophisticated texts. Our task, then, must be to offer children daily earfuls of rich words and patterns. And there is no better source for rich language and sophisticated language structures than quality literature (Hancock 2000; Sorensen & Lehan 1995).

5. *To introduce different genres and writing styles.* For children to make gains in their literacy development, they need not only stronger vocabularies but the ability to navigate a sea of different genres and writing styles. If, for instance, children have never been exposed to, or are unfamiliar with, the genres of an episodic story structure or a sonnet, they will have difficulty reading them; and they will certainly be unable to write them (Meek 1991). By sharing a wide variety of genres and writing styles as read-alouds with children, we will equip them with important experiences and knowledge for making sense of such texts when they encounter them on their own. Furthermore, when children engage in the writing workshop, they will have more choices for writing at their disposal (Stewig 1980). For example, if children have never heard the writing style of William Steig or if they have never been exposed to the genre of the object poem (via, for instance, William Carlos Williams), they will be unable to write like Steig or create object poems of their own. Rather they will be limited by the language patterns at their disposal (Bishop 1998; Smith 1997).

6. *To increase attention span.* As TV works to shorten the attention span of our children, we need a strong antidote. Consider this: On average, children spend 6.2 hours per day watching TV (Postman 1985)—that's more time watching TV than they spend in school. And what they arc watching are programs that incorporate quick visual changes (Healy 1990). For instance, in most television programs the camera shot changes every three to four seconds. Excessive TV viewing habituates children to restlessness, to the expectant idea that they will see something new every few seconds—because they do see something new every few seconds on TV.

TV also promotes passivity; nothing critical or creative is required of the viewer. Viewers are not expected—in fact, are discouraged—from critically analyzing TV content and language or creating unique responses, ideas, or images of their own when viewing (Scheuer 1999). When children read and are read to, however, they enjoy the opposite experience of TV viewing (Marc 1995). Rather that accentuating speed and quick cuts, as does TV, literature read aloud promotes a slow unfolding of events, images, and ideas—items that must take fully embodied shape in the minds of the listeners.

7. *To strengthen cognitive ability.* One way that children strengthen their cognitive abilities is through the adoption and use of increasingly sophisticated language. If their mental faculties are to develop—that is, their ability to reason clearly and to think critically—children must have the means at their disposal to be able to do so (Nell 1994). Such means are found in the language of quality literature. When children regularly listen to the sophisticated language of stories, poetry, and nonfiction—language that they may not have access to in any other way— they slowly assimilate the tools for critical thought and effective cognition (Smith 1997; Temple & Gillet 1996).

8. *To enhance the affective domain.* The chief purpose for the ongoing existence of read-aloud literature is to provide rich aesthetic experiences for the listeners (Cramer & Castle 1994). Not only do listeners create images of settings, characters, objects, and actions in their minds as they read, but they also create intellectual and emotional responses to those images (Fox 1999; Singer & Singer 1990). Through these responses—joy, sadness, suspense, awe, surprise—children come to know the texts they are listening to more fully and they come to know themselves more deeply (Neuman & Celano 2001).

9. *To help second language learners become familiar with the sounds and shapes of English.* By reading aloud to second language learners, we can help them become accustomed to the sound of English and to the way words in English symbolize and communicate meaning. Because the lack of oral language ability in many second language learners inhibits their future literacy efforts, it is essential that we read aloud to them from stories and poems in the language these learners wish to acquire (Hadaway, Vardell, & Young 2001). As second language learners listen to texts read aloud, they will have a language experience that is personally pleasurable and academically important.

10. *To meet national literacy standards.* The International Reading Association and the National Council of Teachers of English (IRA/NCTE) Standards for the English Language Arts encourage students to develop a wide range of literacy capabilities and skills. Essential to the development of all literacy skills—and specifically to the ability to make meaning from encounters with a variety of texts—is access to avenues wherein language can be internalized. When we read aloud to children, we are giving them potent ways to internalize language— because children learn language, and thus internalize it, through the ear. Moreover, reading aloud to children also specifically addresses IRA/NCTE standard no. 11, which asks students to participate in language as knowledgeable, reflective, creative, and critical members of a variety of literacy communities. By reading aloud to children, we allow them to become participants in a literacy community, one that is shaped by their dynamic listening, by their imaginative shaping of the images of the text in their minds, and by their active responses to the texts we share with them.

WHAT TO KNOW: THREE IDEAS TO CONSIDER
BEFORE READING ALOUD

Know What You Like to Read.   The first rule of thumb is to know what you like to read and to share what you like. If you enjoy a story or a poem or a particular piece of nonfiction, you will have a much easier time conveying the essence of the text than trying to "sell" a text that you really don't like. Children tend to know when we're faking it, that is, when we're trying to get them interested in a story or poem that we don't particularly like.

Know the Text.   Children tend to enjoy stories, poems, or pieces of nonfiction that are strong, vivid, and self-contained. In other words, children tend to avoid those texts that are didactic, that have a clear "message." For example, they enjoy stories that are dramatic and suspenseful or silly and humorous. Children love to sit on the edge of their seats and wonder how the main character will get out of a tough situation; they also love to laugh. We can never go wrong when we share stories that create suspense, poems that evoke laughter, or nonfiction that arouses curiosity and wonder.

Know the Audience.   Young children (ages 3 to 7) respond well to texts that have strong language patterns: rhythm, rhyme, repetition, assonance, onomatopoeia, and alliteration. They also enjoy stories that are silly on an elemental and obvious level. Older children (ages 8 to 10) enjoy suspenseful stories where they can identify with the hero or heroine and stories that stretch their imaginations beyond the confines of the everyday world. Tall tales, myths, legends, and folk tales are often among their favorites. And, of course, they also enjoy stories and poems that make them laugh. Children who are moving into adolescence also enjoy stories that allow them to identify with the protagonists, but these stories need to be ones that deal with the problems of the teen years, such as the search for identity, the quest for courage, and the pursuit of integrity. They also respond well to texts that present ideas and issues that are not black or white, but are complex and indeterminate.

For a complete description of how to match children and books, along with book lists, see *Children's Literature in Education* (sixth edition) by Charlotte S. Huck, et al.

Prepare the Text.   Before reading aloud, it is a good idea to practice. Read the text once to gain general knowledge: what is the genre of the text? how is it structured? Read it twice to understand the interworkings of the language and ideas: what are the main ideas? what is most important in the text? what kind of language is being used? are there areas that present some difficulties? Read it a third time with an eye toward how to bring the text to life: what should be emphasized during oral reading? where and when is it necessary to change the voice? Then read the text aloud two or three times to develop fluency, comfort, dramatic emphasis, and vocal variety.

READ-ALOUD RESOURCES

*Indicates especially useful anthologies and collections

Accidents May Happen: Fifty Inventions Discovered by Mistake by Charlotte Foltz Jones
American Children's Folklore edited by Simon J. Bronner
American Indian Trickster Tales selected and edited by Richard Erdoes and Alfonso Ortiz
And the Dish Ran Away with the Spoon by Janet Stevens
Animal Fact, Animal Fable by Semour Simon
*A Bad Case of the Giggles selected by Bruce Lansky
The Book of Dragons selected by Michael Hague
Boston Tea Party by Pamela Duncan Edwards

British Folktales selected by Kevin Crossley Holland
Brown Bear, Brown Bear, What Do You See? by Bill Martin, Jr.
Bugs! by David T. Greenberg
Chinese Fairytales & Fantasies translated and edited by Moss Roberts
Click, Clack, Moo: Cows That Type by Doreen Cronin
Cloudy with a Chance of Meatballs by Judi Barrett
Cowboy Folk Humor: Life and Laughter in the American West by John O. West
The Dancing Skeleton by Cynthia DeFelice
*The Dark Thirty by Patricia McKissack
Days with Frog and Toad by Arnold Lobel
Del Ombligo de la Luna: From the Bellybutton of the Moon by Francisco Alarcon
The Desert Is My Mother by Pat Mora
Dinorella by Pamela Edwards
Don't Know Much about the Presidents by Kenneth C. Davis
The Doorbell Rang by Pat Hutchins
*Extraordinary Origins of Everyday Things by Charles Panati
*Falling Up by Shel Silverstein
*The Family of Stories edited by Anita Moss and Jon C. Stott
Favorite Folktales from Around the World selected and edited by Jane Yolen
Five-Minute Mini-Mysteries by Stan Smith
Food Fight! by Carol Diggory Shields
Frida by Jonah Winter
Frogs by Christine Butterworth
Garbage Delight by Dennis Lee
George Shrinks by William Joyce
The Ghost-Eye Tree by Bill Martin, Jr.
The Giant's Toe by Brock Cole
Green Wilma by Tedd Arnold
Heckedy Peg by Audrey Wood
I Am the Dog, I Am the Cat by Donald Hall
*If I Were in Charge of the World and Other Worries by Judith Viorst
Isabel and the Hungry Coyote by Keith Polette
James and the Giant Peach by Roald Dahl
The Jolly Postman by Janet and Allen Ahlberg
Joseph Had a Little Overcoat by Simms Taback
*Kids Pick the Funniest Poems edited by Bruce Lansky
The Little Mouse, the Red Ripe Strawberry, and the Big Hungry Bear by Audrey Wood
The Little Old Woman Who Was Not Afraid of Anything by Linda Williams
A Little Pigeon Toad by Fred Gwynne
Milo's Hat Trick by Jon Agee
Mississippi River Tales edited by Frank McSherry, Jr., Charles G. Waugh, and Martin Harry Greenberg
Mrs. Biddlebox by Linda Smith
My Life with the Wave by Catherine Cowan
Myths and Legends from Around the World by Sandy Shepherd
*The New Kid on the Block by Jack Prelutsky
No Jumping on the Bed by Tedd Arnold
The Old Man and His Door by Gary Soto
Parts by Tedd Arnold
*Pass the Poetry, Please! edited by Lee Bennett Hopkins
*A Piece of the Wind edited by Patricia McKissack
The Polar Express by Chris Van Allsburg
A Quiet Place by Douglas Wood
*Read-Aloud Poems for Young People: An Introduction to the Magic and Excitement of Poetry edited by
    Glorya Hale

A Ring of Tricksters selected and retold by Virginia Hamilton
Sad Underwear and Other Complications by Judith Viorst
The Scrambled States of America by Laurie Keller
The Secret Knowledge of Grown-ups by David Wisniewski
*The Serpent's Tongue: Prose, Poetry, and Art of the New Mexico Pueblos edited by Nancy Wood
*Sharing Literature with Children: A Thematic Anthology edited by Francelia Butler
The Sixteen Hand Horse by Fred Gwynne
Skunks by David T. Greenberg
Snake Riddles / Spacey Riddles / Mummy Riddles / Creepy Riddles by Katy Hall
*Sol A Sol: Bilingual Poems edited by Lori Marie Carlson
Solomon the Rusty Nail by William Steig
Snowflake Bentley by Jacqueline Briggs Martin
Switch on the Night by Ray Bradbury
A Teacher on Roller Skates and Other School Riddles by David A. Adler
There's an Alligator Under My Bed by Mercer Mayer
This Big Sky by Pat Mora
Tough Cookie by David Wisniewski
A Treasury of Children's Literature edited by Armand Eisen
*A Treasury of Classic Stories for Children selected and retold by Eric Carle
True Lies: 18 Tales for You to Judge by George Shannon
*The 20th Century Children's Book Treasury selected by Janet Schulman
*The 20th Century Children's Poetry Treasury selected by Jack Prelutsky
The Very Hungry Caterpillar by Eric Carle
What They Don't Teach You about History: Hundreds of Peculiar and Fascinating Facts by Tim Wood and Ian Dicks
Where the Wild Things Are by Maurice Sendak
Who Wants a Cheap Rhinoceros? by Shel Silverstein
Wild Birds by Joanne Ryder
Wings by Christopher Myers
The Wise & Foolish Tongue: Celtic Stories & Poems collected and told by Robin Williamson
Workshop by Andrew Clements
The Wolf Is Coming by Elizabeth MacDonald
The Wretched Stone by Chris Van Allsburg
*You Read to Me & I'll Read to You: 20th-Century Stories to Share selected by Janet Schulman
Zathura by Chris Van Allsburg

CHAPTER TWO

READYING CHILDREN TO READ ALOUD

Reasons and Preparations

One way to improve fluency is to provide reading practice. An effective reading practice approach is guided oral reading. This procedure has a positive impact on word recognition, fluency, and comprehension. This is true across a range of grade levels, and it is true for all students.
—National Reading Panel, *Teaching Children to Read*

[T]he literary work exists in the transaction between a reader and a text. The active participatory role of readers encompasses—in conjunction with comprehension—discovering meaning, responding emotionally, developing interpretation. Readers are not passive spectators of the text but active performers with the text.
—Nicholas J. Karolides, "The Reading Process: Transactional Theory in Action"

Expressiveness of oral reading and individual interpretation of text constitutes the core of personal response. Delivery, tone, pitch, and volume become components of expression as the reader strives to share the emotion of the text. Personal interpretation results in individual response as the meaning one derives from the text gives rise to the emotional effort behind the oral interpretation of the text.
—Marjorie R. Hancock, *A Celebration of Literature and Response*

Children are, for the most part, energetic beings who love using words. To listen to them at play is to hear language bubbling and bristling with life. Such language is immediate, brimming with vigor and vitality. The language of children is nearly always an essential act, one painted with bright emotional colors and textured with the grit and grain of specific, self-selected purposes.

Even though children may speak dynamically, they are limited in what they say by the words they have internalized (Fox 1999; Vygotsky 1978). If we want children to internalize rich language, we need to teach them how to translate that dynamism from speech to print, from the way that words are spoken spontaneously to the way that words are read aloud deliberately. In other words, if children don't hear and speak new words, they will never mentally digest them. When children make this transference with practice over time, they will come to infuse what they read aloud with those same urgent energies that they use when they speak. In this way, they will find that reading aloud is an authentic and potent way to discover, create, and express meaning. When children repeatedly read expressively, they will necessarily internalize the language of the texts they are reading (Goodman & Goodman 1994).

When children read aloud without thorough preparation, however, we often hear one of two things. Some children, who are good at decoding, will read a text as quickly as they can; and even though they read without any hint of expression, they do get most of the words "right." Other children, who are not so good at decoding, will frequently stumble across the page, without expression, to haltingly reach the end of the text. As we listen to many children read with expressionless voices, we might wonder: where is the energy and vigor that punctuates their voices when they speak at play? where is the emotion? where is the meaning? where is the fluency? where is the vitality and the intentionality?

One problem that attends such expressionless oral reading is that neither good nor struggling decoders have a full grasp or complete understanding of what they are reading. When most children read aloud (especially if they are reading "cold," with no practice), they comprehend little of what they read. Some readers may catch hold of some content, but most will miss deeper levels of meaning. Typically, as children read aloud, they often concern themselves with denotation and ignore connotation. Overwhelmed by print and unable to read on more than a surface level, many children do not know how to read print material in expressive and meaningful ways—in ways that help them enjoy high levels of fluency, comprehension, and self-confidence. And if children read aloud without fluency or expression, or if they struggle when they read aloud (and thus fail to construct meaning), then too their silent reading will suffer from a corresponding lack of expression and ability to construct meaning (Martens 1997). If we want to help children become stronger readers, we need to teach them—as a key component of our literacy programs—how to read aloud well (Gutiérrez, Baquedano-López, & Turner 1997).

REASONS TO TEACH CHILDREN TO READ ALOUD

1. *To enhance fluency.* Fluency is an essential part of successful reading. Fluency is based on automaticity (a reader's ability to recognize words automatically). If children are to become both automatic and fluent readers, they need practice. Preparing to read a text aloud expressively provides children with the time and means to recognize words automatically and to read a text with a high percentage of accuracy. When children practice by engaging in repeated oral readings, their levels of fluency increase significantly (Rasinski 2000; Martens 1997).

2. *To strengthen comprehension.* When children use techniques for expressive oral reading, their comprehension of what they are reading dramatically increases. Since fluency is closely tied to comprehension, when children become smoother and more accurate readers they will also become more knowledgeable ones. By practicing a text, children will become more familiar with its words, sentence patterns, and organizational structure. Once children become familiar and comfortable with a text, they are then in a position to make discoveries about the different kinds of meanings (both denotative and connotative) that may emerge from their interaction with the text (Apol & Harris 1999). Because they are approaching and envisioning reading anew, children who know how to read expressively show a greater understanding of the texts they have chosen to read (Davis 1997).

3. *To develop critical reading skills.* For children to read expressively, they must make conscious decisions about how to read and what they should emphasize while they are reading so that they can effectively communicate both the surface and deeper meanings of a text. For instance, if children are to read and communicate both the denotative level (content) and the connotative components (emotions and attitudes) of the opening line of Robert Louis Stevenson's "My Shadow" ("I have a little shadow that goes in and out with me"), they must decide what the text is literally saying and what emotions are being implied. Once children have decided what emotions and attitudes are being implied, they will have to decide how to use their voices to communicate those emotions and attitudes (Popp 1996; Barton & Booth 1990). By reading and expressing two levels of the text at once, children have necessarily engaged in critical thinking: they have examined and analyzed the text, made inferences, drawn conclusions, and have made informed decisions about how to vocally communicate those inferences and conclusions (Richards 2000). In this way, children who learn to read aloud expressively will become more sensitive to the workings of print language and will gain insights into what they are reading (Martinez, Roser, & Strecker 1999).

Additionally, when children gather in their reading response groups to rehearse their readings and gain feedback from their peers, they learn how to use critical listening to critique one another's readings. As they give supportive and helpful feedback to each other, children learn that texts are open to interpretation and negotiation, and that meaning is a matter of how one analyzes and performs the text (Enciso & Edmiston 1997).

4. *To develop other important reading skills.* When children prepare to read expressively, they will develop competence in grammar, memory, attention, sequencing, and understanding cause and effect (Healy 1990). Reading well takes time, focus, and attention; and if children are going to read aloud well, they must give the requisite time, focus, and attention to prepare the text. As children prepare a text for oral reading, they will gain a greater understanding of how grammatical and rhetorical structures (sentences, stanzas, and paragraphs) work and how the sequencing of words and ideas plays an important role in the delivery of meaning (Hancock 2000).

5. *To help struggling readers.* When struggling readers learn to use expressive oral reading skills and apply them to something they are going to read aloud, they become stronger readers. By rehearsing their readings through repeated practice, struggling readers improve their accuracy and word recognition abilities (Morado, Koenig, & Wilson 1999).

Additionally, as struggling readers read aloud, they can more effectively monitor themselves. As they read, they can listen to discover if what they are reading "sounds right" and if it makes sense. Moreover, they can also record their readings and listen to themselves; in this way, they can locate areas that need improvement and work on them. By monitoring themselves as they read aloud, struggling readers become more fluent and more confident readers (Armbruster, Lehr, & Osborn 2001).

6. *To build confidence.* When children read with expressive skills, they will also develop more confidence in themselves as readers. No longer limited either to rapid word-calling or to stumbling over print, children will discover that, with practice and guidance, they can become more fluent, purposeful, and effective readers of the kinds of print material that had previously frustrated or befuddled them. And with repeated success, their confidence levels will rise (Davis 1997).

7. *To facilitate collaborative learning.* As children gather together in small groups—Reading Response Groups—to practice their oral readings, they receive feedback from the other members of the group. Through the exchange of ideas about the practice readings, and through the critical feedback that they give one another, children enter into collaborative learning. As children work to assist one another to become stronger expressive readers, they work together to increase the purposefulness of learning: how to connect with one another and how to connect new skills to texts they are choosing to read aloud.

Furthermore, as groups of children learn to use expressive reading skills to read to one another in various venues (i.e., Choral Reading, Shared Reading, and Reader's Theatre), they will naturally step into the oral tradition of literature because they will have taken a large part in creating a community of interested readers and listeners. In such a community, words are relished and the sounds of speech are celebrated. Spoken words again take their rightful place at the fountainhead of communal literacy development (Gutiérrez, Baquedano-López, & Turner 1997).

Additionally, such a community is important because it sustains itself and it is self-supporting (Egan 1997). Since all children are reading aloud in a variety of formats, there are many avenues of support available to them: individual support, buddy support, reading support groups, and whole-group encouragement. When children realize that they are reading expressively in a supportive atmosphere, they will relax, make discoveries, and begin to take risks. In a psychologically safe environment, children will more rapidly take ownership of their reading and learning (Probst 1988).

■ ■ ■ ■ ■

REASONS TO TEACH CHILDREN TO READ ALOUD

1. To enhance fluency.
2. To strengthen comprehension.
3. To develop critical reading skills.
4. To develop other important reading skills.
5. To help struggling readers.
6. To build confidence.
7. To facilitate collaborative learning.
8. To enable second language learners to make gains in English literacy.
9. To share newly crafted abilities with others.
10. To address national literacy standards.

8. *To enable second language learners to make gains in English literacy.* If second language learners are going to develop literacy skills in English, they should engage in repeated practice, they should have scaffolds for learning new words in a meaningful way, and they should use language in a socially interactive way. By teaching second language learners to read aloud expressively, we give them the opportunity to practice the reading selection many times. In the classroom, they practice with, and get feedback from, their Reading Response Groups. Because the groups are small, and because there is a clear response procedure to follow, second language learners will feel freer to take the small risks necessary to managing and mastering a new language. Moreover, through repetition, these learners will begin to assimilate new words and word patterns (Ferguson & Young 1996). When these learners approach new texts, they can learn unfamiliar words in a safe atmosphere; they can work with a reading partner, with members of their Reading Response Groups, or with the teacher. Each of these provides meaningful scaffolds for learning new words (Abbot & Grose 1998). And when these learners present their texts in individual readings, in Reader's Theatre, or in Choral Readings, they will be dramatizing the texts they have chosen in ways that involve social interaction. Through such dramatic, social interactions, these learners will more rapidly internalize the words, structures, and meanings of a second language.

9. *To share newly crafted abilities with others.* Once children learn how to read aloud expressively, they often become so excited that they want to read aloud more often and in more varied situations. As children become better oral readers, they will want to read aloud in the classroom, at home, and for other classes (usually of younger children) in their schools. Moreover, because they have mastered new skills, children who often felt like failures as readers will shine with new excitement as they realize and share their newly built reading expertise with others (Stayter & Allington 1991).

10. *To address national literacy standards.* IRA/NCTE standard no. 4 asks students to adjust their use of spoken, written, and visual language (e.g., conventions, style, vocabulary) to communicate effectively with a variety of audiences and for different purposes. The activities in this book, and especially those in Chapters 4 and 5, are specifically designed to give students the specific skills they will need so that they can share texts that are structured "to communicate effectively with a variety of audiences and for different purposes."

As we lead students through the activities in Chapters 4 and 5, we will also be addressing standard no. 3 which asks students to apply a wide range of strategies to comprehend, interpret, evaluate, and appreciate texts. Each of the activities in Chapter 4 is crafted in such a way that it will guide students to becoming critical listeners of texts read aloud. When we take students through the Focused Anticipation Guide Activity, for instance, we are using an explicit strategy that will enable students "to comprehend, interpret, evaluate, and appreciate" the text we are sharing. Such is the case with the other activities in Chapter 4 as well.

PREPARING CHILDREN TO READ ALOUD

Teaching children to read aloud entails more than inviting them to choose a text and to rehearse reading it. Reading expressively involves a number of discreet factors, all of which can be taught to children. When mastered and combined, these factors will lead children to become more effective oral readers. These factors also provide a means of evaluating how well children read aloud.

Before children tackle a text orally, they need to understand what emotions and attitudes are stated or implied; that is, children need to learn to "get the feel" of a text (Booth & Moore 1988). Through multiple readings and discussions, children will begin to get a sense of a text's emotions. Once children have decided what emotions are present, then they can be taught how to express them through the body and the voice (Richards 2000).

For instance, what emotions are present in these lines by Walt Whitman?

> *O Captain! my Captain! our fearful trip is done,*
> *The ship has weathered every rack, the prize we sought is won,*
> *The port is near, the bells I hear, the people all exulting,*
> *While follow eyes the steady keel, the vessel grim and daring;*
> > *But O heart! heart! heart!*
> > > *O the bleeding drops of red!*
> > > > *Where on the deck my Captain lies*
> > > > *Fallen cold and dead.*

(From "O Captain! My Captain!" in *Leaves of Grass* by Walt Whitman, 1855)

These are not joyful lines; rather they express relief, fear, and shock. And the voice that reads them must communicate those strong emotions. To read aloud effectively, students must learn how to use breath, posture, eye contact, gesture, and vocal variety.

Breath

The first thing that we need to teach children before they read aloud, for example, the poem by Whitman above, is how to work with, and control, the breath. Without breath control, the ability to read with effective vocal variety is nearly impossible. And while breathing may seem to be a simple process, many children are wholly unconscious of how the breath works to produce sound and how to control the breath for better sound production.

Breathing is a two-part process: inhaling, bringing air into the lungs, and exhaling, releasing air from the lungs. To read expressively, one must be able to inhale deeply and calmly and then exhale slowly and deliberately (while making the appropriate vocalizations). When they read aloud (without training), most children do not breathe deeply; rather they only gulp in shallow bits of breath. Often they then experience a shortness of breath; as a result their voices flatten and strain and their oral reading is weak.

Often when children try to breathe deeply, they lift their shoulders, but this does not produce a full inhalation. Instead, we must teach children to breathe with their diaphragms. When we want to fill the lungs we must breathe in and down, not in and up (lifting the shoulders). Two simple exercises will help children breathe more deeply. First, ask children to stand and extend their arms to the sides of their bodies. Direct them to take in a big breath. As they do, they will notice that their stomachs expand as the air fills their lungs. When children breathe in this posture, they will necessarily use abdominal breathing.

Second, ask the children to stand and to place their hands on their stomachs. Tell them to relax their shoulders. Next tell them to tighten their stomach muscles and suddenly force the air out of their lungs; as they do this they should shout "Hah!" Tell them to hold their tightened stomachs for a moment and then quickly relax. They should feel a strong inrush of air. As they breathe in, their stomachs should expand. With this natural and sudden inhalation, they should feel their hands being moved outward by their expanding stomachs. Repeat these exercises; have children practice them until "stomach breathing" becomes easy and natural.

Once children become more familiar with "stomach breathing," they are ready to work with sustained exhalations. Because the amount of breath we release is responsible for the kinds of sounds we produce, we need to teach children how to control and extend their exhalations. Another exercise will assist children in gaining control over how much and how long they breathe out. Give each child a piece of thread (5 to 6 inches in length). Ask children to hold the thread in front of their faces; the thread should be about two inches away from the children's mouths. Ask them to inhale deeply; as they exhale, tell them to count (speaking the words aloud) slowly from one to ten. The thread should flicker with each spoken word (number). The goal is to increase the number of numbers that children can speak before completing their exhalations.

Sustained inhalation and exhalation are central to the production of sound. Children need to gain mastery over this two-part process if they are going to be effective oral readers.

Posture

Poor posture inhibits effective speech while good posture enhances it. Because the way the body is held influences the way the muscles of the chest, throat, and stomach allow for proper breath control, good posture is essential. Teach children to avoid two kinds of postures that work against the ability to control the breath: the slouch and the lean. Sometimes, when reading aloud, children will slouch; their heads drop, their backs sway, and their legs bend at different angles. This posture constricts the breath and makes it impossible for children to use stomach breathing. The other posture to avoid is the lean. Sometimes children are so eager to read aloud that they tighten the muscles in their bodies and crane their bodies forward, bending at the waist. This posture also disallows full inhalation because the muscles are not relaxed and the stomach is continually tight.

The key to good posture is to stand straight, with the shoulders held straight over the top of the body. The head and neck should be relaxed, leaning neither forward nor backward. The entire spine should be relaxed and straight. Legs should also be relaxed; knees should not be locked.

With strong, but relaxed postures, children will find that the body is able to breathe easily and that speech can be produced and manipulated efficiently.

Eye Contact

The key to teaching children to maintain eye contact while they are reading aloud is to help them discover how to make occasional glances at the audience. We want children to become familiar enough with the text they are reading so that they will be able to look up occasionally as they read.

To be able to offer occasional eye contact, children will need to practice their readings. Repeated practice is the key. And the practice sessions should be a lot of short ones, rather than a few long ones. As children practice, their familiarity with the text will grow. As their familiarity grows, they can then decide at what points during the reading they should glance up and establish brief eye contact with the audience. They may even want to mark the text with a pencil or a sticky note to indicate where they should stop and look up.

Gesture

Gestures are tricky. If there are too few, the reading may suffer from lack of physical punctuation; if there are too many, the reading may lose focus. A well-placed gesture can underscore an important idea, while a poorly placed one can diminish the impact of the text. A good rule of thumb to follow is that, when in doubt, it is better to use fewer gestures rather than more.

When teaching children to read, it is often a good idea to teach gesturing last or after children have become at ease with reading aloud. At this point, we can encourage children to avoid using personal and habitual gestures—ones that may have little to do with the texts they are reading. Such gestures do not help express ideas or emotions that are related to the text. In place of habitual gestures, we can teach children to use ones that are more appropriate to expressing ideas and emotions. When children use gestures, however, they must do so in ways that appear natural, not in ways that seem mechanical. Here are some suggestions for a few simple (but certainly not all!) gestures that children might begin using:

arms extended, hands open: to convey honesty or an important idea

arms crossed: to convey fear or anxiety

arm up, finger pointing: to make a point

hand to side of face or forehead: to show concern, shock

head tilted, finger to side of face: to show thought or reflection

hands on sides of face: to show grief or sadness

hand twirling as arm reaches upward: to show exuberance

arms flung wide open: to show happiness

hands clenched at sides of body: to show frustration

fist in front of body: to show anger

arm extended, finger pointing outward in front of body: to show determination or to make a strong point

Vocal Variety

Oftentimes, when we tell children to "read with expression," we don't hear any noticeable improvement. Children fail to read with expression because they don't know what "expression" is. Expression, or vocal variety, is the linchpin of all effective oral reading because it is the music of the voice performing the text. If children are to read aloud well—with expression—they must understand and use all of the elements that comprise vocal variety. "Expression" is a term and an activity that is comprised of seven interlocking parts: volume, pitch, rate, duration, tone, articulation, and emphasis. By teaching children to use these seven components, we can help them become readers who "read with expression."

Volume.   Volume refers to the raising or the lowering of the sound of the voice. Readers use volume by shifting their voices from whispers to shouts. Whispers often indicate suspense, fear, stealth, or quiet anger. Shouts often indicate happiness, anger, shock, or recognition (trying to get someone's attention).

Pitch.   Pitch refers to the raising or lowering of the inflection of the voice. Readers use pitch by shifting their voices from high to low, from a squeak to a bellow—and anywhere in between. A high pitch can indicate shock, surprise, humor, exhilaration, happiness, or relief. A low pitch can indicate anger, seriousness, sadness, worry, mystery, or even deep happiness. For instance, when reading a ghost story, a reader would most likely use a low pitch; when reading a description of a celebration or a victory, a reader might use a higher pitch.

Rate.   Rate refers to the speed at which a sentence or passage in a text is delivered. Higher pitches usually require a faster rate; lower pitches usually require a slower rate. A quick rate of delivery can indicate excitement, anxiety, or fear. A slow rate of delivery can indicate sadness, satisfaction, or confusion. When children read a poem that has rhythm and rhyme, it is essential that they vary the rate of each line to avoid a singsong delivery.

Another aspect of rate is the pause. Pauses are essential as they give the listener time to "catch up" to the content, emotions, or ideas in the text. Pauses also help create suspense. But the key is to decide where to pause and for how long. Most of the time, punctuation marks will tell the reader where to pause. But with poetry, it is sometimes important not to stop at the end of each line or line-break.

Duration.   Duration refers to the time-accent given to a particular word, to how quickly or slowly a word is said. Sometimes it is essential to stretch out the delivery of a word by prolonging the internal vowel sounds (e.g., schooooooool). Stretching out words can indicate deliberation of thought, happiness, playfulness, or seriousness. Quickening the sounds of words, or clipping words short when speaking them can indicate precision, certainty, anger, or seriousness.

Tone.   Tone refers to vocal quality. Examples of tone include nasal, gravelly, hollow, scratchy, screechy, whispery, whiny, or solid. It is important to choose the tone that best expresses the ideas and emotions in the text that is to be read aloud. For instance, if a reader is reading "Casey at the Bat," he or she would probably not want to use a nasal or whiny tone because those tones don't enhance the suspense of the poem.

Articulation.   Articulation refers to the kind of pronunciation that the words of a text receive. Clearly pronounced words are important for effective oral reading. If words are smeared over or run together, the reader will not be understood. Readers must instead shape the sounds of words accurately. Especially important sounds to shape clearly are plosives (p, b, t, d, k, and g in words such as asked, taught, tenth, proud, and bat) and fricatives (f, s, v, z, and ch and sh in such words as fast, super, vivid, zebra, child, and should).

Emphasis.   Emphasis refers to the stress that a word or phrase receives from the reader. The right emphasis makes all the difference. Usually emphasis should be placed on (in this order) verbs, nouns, adverbs, adjectives, pronouns, prepositions, and conjunctions. But phrases can also receive emphasis: participial, gerund, infinitive, absolute, appositive, prepositional. For instance, notice the subtle differences of meaning when the emphasis is shifted in each of the following lines:

I'll take those ruby slippers, my dear.

I'll *take* those ruby slippers, my dear.

I'll take *those* ruby slippers, my dear.

I'll take those *ruby* slippers, my dear.

I'll take those ruby *slippers*, my dear.

I'll take those ruby slippers, *my* dear.

I'll take those ruby slippers, my *dear*.

By using these seven components, the skills of vocal variety, children can make great improvements in their expressive reading abilities. By knowing what a text is designed to communicate and by applying these skills to the act of reading the text aloud, children will be able to read authentically and to share ideas and emotions in ways that may have previously eluded them. The key to using these skills is variety; the reader must combine them seamlessly, without emphasizing one over the other.

APPLYING VOCAL VARIETY SKILLS TO TEXTS

To use vocal variety when reading, children might want to think of the text as a piece of music; in place of notes, however, are words. Just as a musician brings to life the notes on the page, so too will the children make vocal music from the words of the text. If children are to perform the text, they will need to make notations that indicate where they are going to use the skills of vocal variety. To that end, it will be beneficial if children mark the text with a pencil or with sticky pad sheets and use symbols that indicate where they will change the volume and pitch; where they will slow down, speed up, and pause; which words will be elongated and shortened; and what tone of voice they will use. They will also want to make note of any words that will require special attention for the sake of articulation.

The following symbols are suggested for children to use when marking the text:

loud volume:	L	soft volume:	(s)
high pitch:	∧	low pitch:	V
fast rate:	(f)	slow rate:	(sl)
pause:	/		
long duration:	<	short duration:	>
emphasis:	_____		

Here's how a text looks after it has been marked with the vocal variety notations:

Dumpty Down (entire poem to be read with a somber tone)
    V
Humpty Dumpty had a great fall (sl).
He waffled, / toppled, / <fell< / —splat!—from the wall.
       Λ   L
As his jagged pieces / besplattered the ground (sr),
Not a single shell-shocked onlooker uttered a sound.
                           (sl   )
<All< the king's horses / and all the king's men
Silently gazed at the goo; / they were crestfallen.
              V
The king looked down, / gave a small egg salute,
And sighed as he said, / "He needed a parachute."
              (sl   )

Another way to mark a text for expressive readings would be to use colored highlighters. The color red could indicate "loud," yellow–"soft," green–"long duration," and so on.

It is important to guide children through the notation process repeatedly. After they see first how you mark and perform a text a few times, then they will be better prepared to be guided through the process themselves.

First, you should put your marked text on the overhead (or on a poster-sized chart) and then read it aloud so that the children can see how the notations correspond to your vocal variety. After you have demonstrated the notation technique a number of times, you might then place an unmarked text on the overhead and read it aloud using the vocal variety skills. Ask the children to tell you where your volume, pitch, and rate changed; where you paused; and what words you elongated and shortened. By doing this, you will help the children develop an ear that is attuned to the skills of vocal variety.

Additionally, you might want to use the Call and Response technique at this point. As you read aloud a poem a line at a time, and the children mimic your reading, let them know where and why you are applying the particular skills of vocal variety.

READING RESPONSE GROUPS

Once you have familiarized children with the notation system, invite them to select a brief text to prepare to read aloud. Let them work in pairs when they begin marking the text; they should talk to each other about how to mark the text and why. After they have each marked the text, they should read aloud to each other; in this way, they can rehearse their readings. Such rehearsals, or practice sessions, are essential if children are to become comfortable, confident, and knowledgeable when they read aloud (Cramer & Castle 1994).

After they have marked and shared the text, the children should move to Reading Response Groups (four children per group). Reading Response Groups are an essential part of the oral reading process because they allow children to receive constructive feedback, to gain further control over their reading, and they provide a scaffolding for further learning (Johns & VanLeirsburg 1994). Each child reads his or her marked selection in the Reading Response

Groups, using vocal variety. The other members of the group give feedback based on how the text was read. Their feedback should follow the P.Q.P. method: Praise, Question, Polish.

As the reader listens, the other group members should begin by offering specific, positive feedback (praise), which consists of a discussion of the skills of vocal variety; for example, "Your volume changes were great; when you said the word 'splat' real loud, that made a great impact." Next, the listeners ask questions about the reading (question): "Why did you pause at the end of the first line?" "Why did you raise your pitch on the third word?" Finally, the listeners should use the skills of vocal variety to offer revisions or suggestions (polish): "You might want to speed up the rate on the third line or you might want to pause after the third word in the first line." When children respond in these ways, they are developing critical listening skills: no longer focusing solely on content, they are now attending to how effectively the text was conveyed and how, specifically, it might be improved.

One important note: the full use of the notation and performance activity is best suited for children who are capable of reading and understanding texts on their own, that is, children who are (roughly) 8+ years of age. For younger children, it will be most effective to teach them to use one vocal variety skill at a time and to spend a good deal of time on that skill. For instance, when teaching children who are ages 5 to 7 to use vocal variety, it will be effective to teach them one skill per week: teach children, for example, to change the pitch of their voices one week, and practice that skill several times throughout the week—via the Call and Response and the Choral Reading techniques—before teaching the next skill.

EVALUATION

You can use the vocal variety skills to create a form to evaluate the reading performance of children. Each skill is a specific part of the evaluation form and is assigned a point value; as children read, you can then determine which skills the children have mastered and which they need to continue to work on. You can also include other components in the scoring guide such as posture, gestures, and eye contact.

The evaluation form is equitable because it lets the children know precisely how they will be evaluated, and it eliminates as much subjectivity as possible. It is a good idea to distribute the evaluation form to the children at the beginning of the oral reading lesson; that way they will know what they have to do to earn a high score. Moreover, the items on the evaluation form are the same skills that the children will practice at home and discuss in their Reading Response Groups.

One final idea: make a poster of the oral reading skills and display it so that children can be reminded of how they need to listen when you read aloud to them and what they need to do when they read aloud.

ORAL READING REMINDER

Remember to:

- breathe calmly and deeply
- have straight and relaxed posture

- make some eye contact
- use gestures
- change your volume (loud and soft)
- vary your pitch (high and low)
- vary your rate (speed up and slow down)
- find places to pause
- stretch out some vowel sounds
- use the best tone of voice: nasal, hollow, firm, gravelly, screechy, whispery, somber, etc.
- emphasize key words
- pronounce all important consonants

ORAL READING EVALUATION FORM

Does the Reader:

_____   breathe calmly and deeply?

_____   have straight and relaxed posture?

_____   make some eye contact with the audience?

_____   use some gestures to emphasize the meanings of words, phrases, and/or sentences?

_____   change the volume (loud and soft)?

_____   vary the pitch (high and low)?

_____   vary the rate (speed up and slow down)?

_____   find effective places to pause?

_____   stretch out some vowel sounds to emphasize the emotions suggested by certain words?

_____   use an appropriate tone of voice: nasal, hollow, firm, gravelly, screechy, whispery, somber, high-pitched, etc.?

_____   emphasize key words (verbs, nouns, adjectives, adverbs)?

_____   pronounce consonants clearly?

Comments:

CHAPTER THREE

HOW TO READ ALOUD TO CHILDREN

Techniques That Promote Active and Critical Listening

The single most important activity for building reading success is reading aloud to children. Reading aloud should be emphasized not only in the home but also in the classroom, continuing throughout grades K through 12.
—Richard C. Anderson, *Becoming a Nation of Readers: The Report of the Commission on Reading*

A major advantage for children who have the opportunity to listen to stories is that they become used to the language employed in them and don't find stories strange when they begin to read for themselves.
—Frank Smith, *Reading Without Nonsense*

Reading to students and discussing the nature of the reading allows us to focus on the flexible attitude readers need to bring to the reading act. Fluent and understandable reading, not fast reading, is the goal.
—Timothy V. Rasinski, "Speed Does Matter in Reading"

Language without voice is unthinkable.
—Paul Zumthor, *Oral Poetry*

The following techniques can help teachers and parents read aloud successfully to children. Effective oral reading is not simply a matter of opening a book and giving voice to the words on the page, hoping that children will listen. Rather, it involves making deliberate choices about how to prepare children for active and critical listening. Frequently, when children listen to a text read aloud, they may enjoy the experience, but their minds may not be as fully engaged as possible. Our goal is to engage the minds (and hearts!) of children as fully as possible when we read aloud (Fox 1993). One way to help children bring more mind to bear when they listen to us read to them is to let them know the kinds of things they should listen for—things they would most likely not think of on their own. By using the following techniques, we can help children discover many new ways to listen actively and critically to texts. When children learn to listen actively and critically, they will also find new, dramatic, and meaningful avenues into the world of spoken literature.

TOUR GUIDE

While it is always a good idea to read a text straight through from beginning to end, it is also a good idea to stop occasionally to reread a passage and to stop and alert listeners to upcoming passages (Whyte 1994). When we stop to reread or to alert listeners, we are helping our listeners become aware of how language works to create a setting, describe a character, describe an object or action, or present ideas in new ways. In other words, we might think of ourselves as tour guides (Pressley 1998). As we lead our listeners into the world of the text, we need to sometimes stop and point out to them things they might miss if they weren't invited to look for them. If we fail to stop and reread, to point out word-vistas along the tour, we are not giving our listeners the opportunity to catch sight of the interworkings of language.

When children listen to texts read aloud, it is sometimes like watching a train pass at a railroad crossing: if the train is moving too fast, the viewer doesn't have a chance to see the cars whirring by. When we stop and reread, we are giving our listeners a chance to look carefully at some of the wordy "railroad cars" that just flew by.

The same is true when we stop and point out a passage that we are going to read. By letting our listeners know that an important passage or a passage rich in description is forthcoming, they can alter their expectations and change their perspectives. Through such alterations, the listeners can ready themselves to listen more carefully and more critically.

Tour Guide Process No. 1

1. Choose a passage (or an entire text); read aloud for a few moments.
2. Stop and say something like, "You know, that sentence (or paragraph or stanza) that I just read was so wonderful that I want to read it again." For instance, if you are reading *Zeke Pippin* by William Steig, you might stop after you have read the description of Zeke making his way through the dark, tangled forest after his escape from the trio of villainous dogs, and say, "Wow, that description was so powerful that I just have to read it again!"
3. Read the passage again.

Tour Guide Process No. 2

1. Choose a passage (or an entire text); read aloud briefly.
2. Stop and say something like, "This next sentence (or stanza or paragraph) is really wonderful; it contains a great metaphor (or simile, or alliteration, or onomatopoeia, or hyperbole, etc.). For instance, after reading the title, "Zeke Pippin," we might stop and say, "I'd like you to really listen to the opening sentence of this story. It contains some vivid verbs (i.e., 'moseying' and 'rumbling')."

3. Read the passage, emphasizing the elements you want listeners to pay particular attention to.

Tour Guide Variation

Invite your listeners to stop you occasionally while you are reading aloud and ask to hear you
reread a passage or bit of dialogue. Also, ask your listeners to make predictions as to when they
think a particularly noteworthy passage is coming.

Another variation is to use books on tape; play the audiotape of a text while children
follow along silently in their books.

THINK ALOUD

One way to help all children develop stronger reading skills is to acquaint them with the
thought processes that effective readers use when they read (Harvey & Goudvis 2000; Temple
& Gillet 1996). Most children, who are still developing various cognitive abilities, need to
acquire a variety of comprehension strategies if they are to be able to read and understand ever
more sophisticated stories, poems, and nonfictional works. The Think Aloud technique shows
children that reading is a process that requires the reader to think about the text and to construct
meaning as she or he reads (Early & Ericson 1988). When using the Think Aloud technique,
the oral reader says what he or she is thinking about while reading; by expressing his or her
thoughts aloud, the reader demonstrates how the process of comprehending and making meaning is achieved. During a Think Aloud, the oral reader is also able to talk about those things that
all readers need to consider while reading: free and personal associations, discoveries, predictions, mental images evoked by the text, key text features (titles, headings, words, sentences,
figurative language), the way the text connects with prior knowledge, and ways to overcome
problems encountered while reading (Bruner 1979).

Think Aloud Process

1. Choose a text; begin reading aloud.
2. Stop reading after a few moments and voice some personal associations. They need not
   be connected with explicit reading skills or with the interworkings of the text; they
   should be wholly personal and random. Making personal associations lets children
   know that as we read, we all make connections that have little or nothing to do with the
   text—and that it is okay to have and to acknowledge such associations.

   For instance, if you are reading *Heckedy Peg* by Don and Audrey Wood, you
   might introduce the book by making free associations with the title: "I've never heard
   the word 'Heckedy' before, but it reminds me of a boy I knew in grade school whose last
   name was Reckedy. And the word 'Peg' might be short for Peggy, but it also makes me
   think of a wooden peg."
3. At this point, ask the children if they have any personal associations to add to yours.
   Accept all answers, no matter how random or peculiar.
4. When you arrive at a spot in the text that is troublesome (one that is ambiguous or has a
   difficult word or sentence) or that requires further thought, stop and think aloud by

focusing on ways to make sense of the passage in question. For instance, after reading the opening lines from *Heckedy Peg,* you might stop and make such comments as: "The opening line reminds me that nearly all folktales begin with a standard, formulaic opening. This kind of opening lets the reader know that he or she is entering the world of folklore." You can continue with: "Since I know that *Heckedy Peg* is a folktale, I need to remember what I know about folktales: they are usually short stories; they usually have brief introductions; they present the action immediately; they usually have characters that are exact opposites of each other; they sometimes have magic; they were originally handed down orally; they don't have lengthy description of characters or settings; characters are not like real people; and the problems in these stories are usually a conflict of person versus person." As you continue reading the story, you might stop after the section where the children disobey their mother's wishes. Then state: "In folktales, there are many examples of characters who disobey strict orders or instructions." As you continue reading, stop when you arrive at the section where the mother enters the dark forest; you might say: "Now the mother is entering the forest; I wonder how the forest looks? I'll bet it is thick with trees and that the trees blot out the sky and that their branches reach down as if to grab you!" Invite the children to add descriptions. Finally, when you get to the part of the story where the mother is given a chance to redeem her children, who have been turned into food, you might stop and say, "Wow, I wonder how the mother will solve this problem?" Then invite the children to speculate.

5. Put the children in groups of three or four and ask them to perform a Think Aloud with books they have chosen. Remind them that they should focus on the following:
   - personal associations
   - prior knowledge
   - predictions
   - mental images
   - key text features
   - ways of making sense of difficult passages

Think Aloud Variation

As you are reading aloud, sometimes it will be beneficial to stop and ask your listeners what they are thinking about a particular passage (sentence, paragraph, or stanza) that you just read. Invite them to talk about their associations, prior knowledge, predictions, mental images, key text features, or ways that they made sense of the passage.

PICTURE THIS

If children are to make gains in reading enjoyment and in comprehension, they must learn to generate mental images, especially as they read fiction and poetry (Gambell 1993). Not only do readers remember more of what they read when they construct mental images, but they also lay the ground for using inferential thinking skills. Children also discover that, through the construction of mental images, reading is a personal and creative activity (Sinatra 1994). For instance, no two readers will construct the same images based on a story or a poem; consequently, as readers discuss the images they created (and discover that all images, even if they are different and connected to the text, are correct), they will see how critical imagination and inferential thought play key roles in the creation of image-based meaning (Iser 1990).

Picture This Process

1. Select a passage that contains a strong and vivid description of a person, place, or event. The passage should be brief; it should take one to two minutes to read aloud.
2. Before you read aloud, ask the listeners to get ready to create pictures in their minds of what is going to be described. Remind the listeners that creating mental images is an essential part of reading comprehension and that each person will make a slightly different picture or will focus on different aspects of what is being described.
3. Read aloud; pause briefly after each sentence.
4. When you have finished reading, ask the children to describe what they saw in their minds.
5. Record the descriptions of what the listeners imagined. Make note of the similarities and the differences.
6. Ask the children to work in pairs or groups. Using the same book, or different books, invite the children to share among themselves the images they created as they read. Remind the children that it is important to create mental images whenever they read fiction and poetry.

Picture This Variation

After you have read a passage, invite your listeners to act out the scene without using any words. Remind them that in their scenario they must display pertinent ideas and emotions.

Another idea is to invite children to use images to convey their understanding of new vocabulary. Ask them to draw or find pictures (in magazines, newspapers, or catalogues) that display the meanings of the words they have looked up.

RICH LANGUAGE

While many children read fiction and poetry to gain an understanding of the surface elements—content and events—it is important for them to develop an appreciation for the language that conveys those events. Such an appreciation will deepen their understanding of the texts they are reading and move them to the connotative level of reading. When children regularly read with an eye toward the rich language of a text, they will also strengthen their own writing. Reading aloud and asking children to listen not only for plot and action (event) elements, but also for the rich language used to convey those elements, will go a long way in helping children enhance their sensitivity to language (Sanders 1995).

Rich Language Process

(See the Writer's Tools in Chapter 5 for examples.)

1. Select a text that contains many examples of rich language: concrete (not abstract) words, parallel constructions, similes, metaphors, hyperbole, alliteration, onomatopoeia, assonance, repetition, etc.
2. Ask children to jot down (in their writer's notebooks) or note the rich language in the text that you will be reading.
3. As you read, stop and point out a few initial examples of rich language. For instance, if you read *Owl Moon* by Jane Yolen, point out the richness of the opening similes and metaphors.
4. Continue reading aloud; read slowly enough so that children can catch the rich language.
5. Ask children to share their discoveries.

Rich Language Variation

As children read self-selected texts silently, ask them to record in their writer's notebooks examples of rich language that they encounter. This type of recording can be done throughout the year.

PUNCTUATION POWER

To help children learn how the proper deployment of punctuation marks helps readers process the language of a text so that they can more easily make meaning, use the Punctuation Power technique. Children may not know, for instance, that a comma signals a pause; that a period signals a longer pause (and the end of a complete thought); that a question mark signals the need to raise the pitch of the voice at the end of a sentence; that an exclamation mark signals the need to raise the volume of the voice at the end of the sentence; and that underlined, italicized, or bold-faced words require special emphasis. The Punctuation Power technique will help children learn the purpose of various text signals.

Punctuation Power Process

1. Choose a brief paragraph to read aloud.
2. Read the paragraph aloud without pausing at commas or periods; do not change the inflection or volume of your voice for question marks or exclamation marks or words that require special emphasis.
3. Ask the children if the passage made sense.
4. Read the passage aloud again, this time more slowly. Ask children to raise their hands at points where they think you should pause and add a comma; stop and add a period; or change the pitch or volume of your voice to add a question mark, an exclamation point, or to place special emphasis.

5. Display the passage, without punctuation marks, on an overhead transparency. Go through the passage, phrase by phrase and sentence by sentence, and invite the children to tell you where and why to insert punctuation marks. (You might want to present mini-lessons, if necessary, on punctuation marks at this point.)

Punctuation Power Variation

As you read aloud a text that has no punctuation and is displayed on the overhead projector, invite children to use hand signals to indicate where punctuation marks belong: one hand in the air for commas, arms folded for periods, two hands in the air for exclamation marks, arms extended in front with palms upturned for question marks, and arms extended to the sides for special emphasis words.

FOCUSED ANTICIPATION GUIDES

One reason why children often fail to achieve high levels of comprehension after they have read a text is that they didn't know what they should have paid attention to while they were reading (Smith 1997). Most often, children read on the denotative level, that is, they read to understand plot in fiction, actions and events in poetry, and a scattering of factual content in nonfiction. They do not usually know how to organize their expectations regarding what they are going to read, and they do not know what textual material is important—that is, what material they should attend to so that they can construct meaning.

The responses children often make to most texts are personal, having to do with nontextual associations that connect to their previous experiences and prior knowledge. These kinds of responses do not usually link up to the text on more than a surface level, and they do not help children understand the text on its own terms. If we want children to read more deeply (and to listen more critically) and to comprehend the text based on either the elements of fiction, poetic structures, or nonfictional schema, we need to guide them into doing so. And such guidance must be furnished before students read, not after (Adams 1994).

When we use the Focused Anticipation Guide technique, we are helping students to read much more effectively, comprehend more deeply, and develop metacognition (becoming aware of their thinking and various textual elements as they read) because we are showing them how to discover precisely what they should look for as they read (Tierney, John, & Dishner 1995). As children use Focused Anticipation Guides to ground their predictions about texts they are going to read, they discover that they also have a greatly increased interest in wanting to read—and they want to read so that they can find out, that is, so that they can verify their predictions. Focused Anticipation Guides build in children a strong need to know.

Focused Anticipation Guide Process

1. Choose a text to read.

2. Create a Focused Anticipation Guide by constructing a series of statements about specific items in the text; some of the statements should be true, and some false. For fiction, each statement should contain an embedded reference to one of the elements of fiction. For poetry, each statement should contain an embedded reference to the elements of poetry. And for nonfiction, each statement should refer to a statement of factual content.

3. Either display the cover of the book you are going to share or read the opening paragraph and ask the children to answer each statement before they read with either yes, no, or maybe. The emphasis here is not on "right" answers; we are not asking the children to make correct predictions. We simply want them to use the statements to form a working hypothesis about the text they are going to hear.

4. Read the text aloud. As you read, ask children to let you know when they have found the correct answer to each statement. You will have to read slowly and stop at places in the text that correspond to each of the statements in the Focused Anticipation Guide. For instance, after reading the exposition of *The Dark at the Top of the Stairs* by Sam McBratney, it should be evident that the story is set inside; at this point, stop and ask the children if the story has connected with any of their statements on the Focused Anticipation Guide. The children should let you know that they heard that the story was not set outside. It will be effective if you have the Focused Anticipation Guide on a transparency so that you can put the correct answers that the children give you in the "after" reading spaces.

5. Here are four sample Focused Anticipation Guides:

FICTION: *ISABEL AND THE HUNGRY COYOTE* BY KEITH POLETTE

Directions: After each statement in the "before" reading space, place Y (yes) if you think the statement is true, N (no) if you think the statement is not true, and M (maybe) if you can't decide whether the statement is true or untrue.

The story will take place outside (setting).	before _____	after _____
Isabel will be the main character (protagonist).	before _____	after _____
Coyote will be the opposing character (antagonist).	before _____	after _____
Isabel and the Coyote will talk (dialogue).	before _____	after _____
Isabel won't want to visit her grandmother (motivation).	before _____	after _____
Isabel will be brave (character trait).	before _____	after _____
Isabel will be trapped in the desert (problem).	before _____	after _____
Isabel will solve the problem by herself (resolution).	before _____	after _____
There will be repetition in the story (language).	before _____	after _____
There will be danger in the story (thematic motif).	before _____	after _____

FICTION: *ZATHURA* BY CHRIS VAN ALLSBURG

Directions: After each statement in the "before" reading space, place Y (yes) if you think the statement is true, N (no) if you think the statement is not true, and M (maybe) if you can't decide whether the statement is true or untrue.

Walter and Danny will be the protagonists (main characters).	before _____	after _____
Aliens will be the antagonists (opposing characters).	before _____	after _____
There will be no dialogue in the story (dialogue).	before _____	after _____
Similes and metaphors will be used (figurative language).	before _____	after _____
Alliteration will be used (figurative language).	before _____	after _____
The story will be set in outer space (setting).	before _____	after _____
Walter and Danny will feel only two emotions (emotions).	before _____	after _____
The story will be told in the first person (point of view).	before _____	after _____
Walter and Danny will change in the story (character).	before _____	after _____
Conflict will be person versus person (conflict).	before _____	after _____
Conflict will be person versus self (conflict).	before _____	after _____
Conflict will be person versus society (conflict).	before _____	after _____
Walter and Danny will go on a circular journey (story structure).	before _____	after _____
Walter and Danny will seek help to resolve conflict (problem resolution).	before _____	after _____

POETRY: "THE NEW KID ON THE BLOCK" BY JACK PRELUTSKY

Directions: After each statement in the "before" reading space, place Y (yes) if you think the statement is true, N (no) if you think the statement is not true, and M (maybe) if you can't decide whether the statement is true or untrue.

The poem will rhyme (rhyme).	before _____	after _____
The poem will contain similes and metaphors (figurative language).	before _____	after _____
The poem will contain alliteration (figurative language).	before _____	after _____
The poem will talk about and name "feelings" (content).	before _____	after _____
The poem will be written in the first person (point of view).	before _____	after _____

The poem will have many abstract nouns (language).	before _____	after _____
The poem will tell a story (type of poem: lyric or narrative).	before _____	after _____
The poem will have a serious tone (tone).	before _____	after _____

NONFICTION: *BUTTERFLIES* BY DONNA BAILEY

Directions: After each statement in the "before" reading space, place Y (yes) if you think the statement is true, N (no) if you think the statement is not true, and M (maybe) if you can't decide whether the statement is true or untrue.

Some butterflies have two sets of wings.	before _____	after _____
Monarch butterflies hibernate during the winter.	before _____	after _____
A butterfly's wings are covered with tiny scales.	before _____	after _____
Many butterflies are brightly colored to warn their enemies that they are dangerous to eat.	before _____	after _____
Some butterflies have eyes on their wings that help them see when they fly.	before _____	after _____
Moths and butterflies use their wings the same way.	before _____	after _____

Focused Anticipation Guide Variation

Rather than ask children to make decisions about specific items for specific stories, invite them to complete the following generic Focused Anticipation Guide. This guide can be used (and modified) to fit any story.

FOCUSED ANTICIPATION GUIDE

Directions: Before reading any story, complete the following: After each statement in the "before" reading space, place Y (yes) if you think the statement is true, N (no) if you think the statement is not true, and M (maybe) if you can't decide whether the statement is true or untrue.

The story will have an elaborate exposition.	before _____	after _____
The protagonist will be fully developed and reveal numerous conflicting emotions and desires.	before _____	after _____
The story will present examples of opposites.	before _____	after _____
The conflict will be person versus person.	before _____	after _____
The conflict will be person versus nature.	before _____	after _____

The point of view will be first person.	before _____	after _____
The setting will be unimportant.	before _____	after _____
The story will have a surprise ending.	before _____	after _____
The antagonist will be _____. (Fill in this blank with whomever you think the antagonist might be.)	before _____	after _____
The protagonist will be motivated chiefly by fear.	before _____	after _____
The story will have a happy ending.	before _____	after _____
The protagonist will resolve the conflict without help.	before _____	after _____
The theme will be: "Be careful what you wish for."	before _____	after _____

F.I.R.E.

If students are to become active, involved readers, they need strategies that will help them understand how to perform the kinds of readings that texts ask of them and how to become the kinds of readers that texts need them to be (Almasi 2003). Such strategies, therefore, should enable students to draw upon, and think meaningfully about, their prior knowledge before they read (and thus help them find ways to illuminate the strands and facets of those things they have ignored or forgotten), engage in a predictive and hypothetical dialogue with the text they are going to read, connect what they know with what they are reading, recognize the variety of meaning-making choices available to them as readers, and assimilate what they have read so that they may use it as prior knowledge in future contexts (Polette 1998). F.I.R.E. (Forecast, Identify, Read/React/Respond, Explain/Elaborate) is just such a process that allows children to interact with a story before they read it and to construct ideas about what the story could contain.

F.I.R.E. Process

1. Choose a fictional text (picture storybook, short story, or junior novel).

2. Decide what elements of fiction and/or aspects of fictional language you want the children to predict. Place them in the F.I.R.E. grid (page 34).

3. Ask children to make predictions based on the general categories that you have furnished in the preceding step. Children must then generate specific items that could be placed beneath each heading. For example, if you were to share *The Stonecutter* by Gerald McDermott, you would ask children to examine the cover illustration and then think of specific items that could be placed within the F.I.R.E. grid categories. If you were to share a novel such as *Holes* by Louis Sachar, you would ask the children to read the first two or three pages and then think of specific items that could be placed in the categories. To complete this part of the activity, which will focus their reading, children

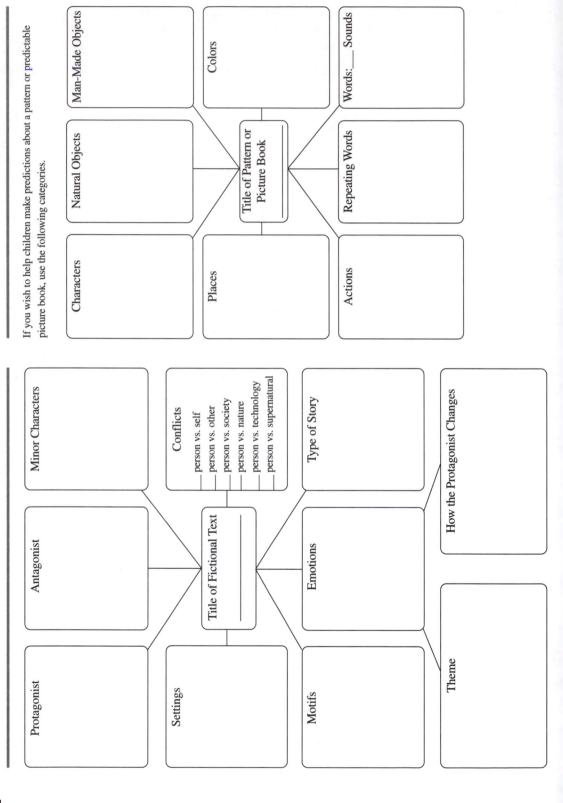

F. I. R. E.

Protagonist

Antagonist

Minor Characters

Title of Fictional Text
_____

Settings

Conflicts
person vs. self
person vs. other
person vs. society
person vs. nature
person vs. technology
person vs. supernatural

Type of Story

Emotions

Motifs

How the Protagonist Changes

Theme

F. I. R. E. Variation

If you wish to help children make predictions about a pattern or predictable picture book, use the following categories.

Characters

Natural Objects

Man-Made Objects

Title of Pattern or Picture Book
_____

Places

Colors

Actions

Repeating Words

Words:____ Sounds

must make hypotheses about key aspects of the story that are grounded in the elements of fiction. This activity helps children discover precisely what they should take note of as they read and teaches them how the elements of fiction are integral components of every story.

4. Lead the children through the activity by following the four F.I.R.E. steps:

   F: *Forecast:* After you have examined the cover illustration (or after you have read the opening paragraph of a story or the first two to three pages of a novel), make some preliminary decisions about the "elements" that you think the story might contain (i.e., the "elements of fiction"). Put whatever ideas you have in each box. Feel free to be as divergent as you wish.

   I: *Identify:* Identify those items about which you are fairly confident by placing a "Y" (yes) next to them; identify those items about which you are not so confident—those you are only "guessing" about—by placing an "M" (maybe) next to them. (The object is not to try and be "correct." There are no right or wrong answers at this stage.)

   R: *Read/React/Respond:* As you read, put words or short phrases next to those items that have an "M" next to them—these words and phrases should serve as brief responses/clarifications/revisions.

   E: *Explain/Elaborate:* Explain how your predictive "chart" compares to the story; be sure to make note of those specific items that your chart has in common with the story and those that it does not.

K-THIK CHART

Children often need explicit guidance when they read nonfiction. Nonfiction, which is structured differently from fiction, does not furnish children with the ready-to-grip handles of character and plot. Because they don't have characters and plotlines to guide them, many children have difficulty sustaining their interest in, and their understanding of, nonfiction. Frequently, when they read nonfiction, children are overwhelmed with data, with factual material; and being overwhelmed, they don't know what data to remember because they don't know what data is important. One reason why children don't know what data to remember when they read nonfiction is because they haven't established a clear purpose for reading (Gambrell 1999). Using the K-ThIK Chart will provide children with both a self-generated purpose for reading nonfiction—to verify their hypotheses—and with a way to let them know what data to remember (Kutz & Roskelly 1991). As such, when we read the text aloud, children will know precisely what to listen for, and they will have a keen desire to do so. (K-ThIK stands for "what I Know and what I THink I Know.)

K-ThIK Process

1. Choose a nonfictional text.
2. Before reading, ask children to list everything they know about the topic of the text you have chosen and everything they think they know. (It will be helpful if you give the

children categorical headings beneath which they can place their knowledge and their speculations.)

3. On an overhead transparency, list everything the children know on one side and everything they think they know on the other side (encourage children to make guesses about what they think they know). The goal here is not necessarily to elicit correct answers from children, but to gather up their ideas and speculations.

4. Read the text aloud. As you come to various data in the text, ask children to eliminate or correct the data that they gave you, which you recorded on the overhead transparency.

5. Here's a sample K-ThIK Chart for *Leonardo da Vinci* by Diane Stanley:

What I Know	What I Think I Know
birthplace	
birth date	
personality traits	
goals	
fears	
interests	
inventions	
discoveries	
friends	
rivals	
travels	

K-ThIK Variation

Prior to sharing a nonfictional text, ask children to make predictions as to what kinds of content the text will contain. For instance, if you are going to share an article on the history of hot air ballooning, invite the children to speculate as to the kinds of facts the article will contain (e.g., about the time and place of invention, the inventors, first flight, first passengers, balloon materials).

SELECTIVE READING

Good readers make continuous predictions while they read, and their predictions are based on the ongoing clues that the text provides (Pressley 1998). When reading fiction, for example, good readers are constantly on the lookout for how a character's actions, speech, desires, and fears influence the plot and conflict. Good readers also understand that what comes first in a text will usually be connected to, or motivate, what comes later (Smith 1997). Many children, however, do not make such predictions because they have not yet learned how to gather such clues and use them as guides for their reading. The Selective Reading technique offers children a chance to use textual clues that appear in the beginning of a story so that they can make the kinds of predictions they need to become more motivated, self-directed readers.

Selective Reading Process

1. Choose a story; folktales work especially well.
2. Read aloud only the first sentence in the first five or six paragraphs. You may need to do this part of the activity two or three times.
3. Ask the children to tell you what they heard. Record their responses, differentiating between fact and opinion, on an overhead transparency (this might be a place for a mini-lesson on fact and opinion; see the example at the end of this activity). Focus on setting, character (types of characters and their desires and fears), plot, point of view, and conflict.
4. Ask the children to make predictions about the story based on what they already know and what they think they know (which you recorded in the previous step. Who might the main character be? Who might the opposing character be? What might the main character both want and fear? Where might the story be set? From what point of view will the story be told? Will the conflict be person versus person, person versus self, person versus society, person versus nature, person versus technology, and/or person versus supernatural? Will the main character achieve or obtain what he or she wants? Will the main character have to give up something to achieve or obtain his or her goals?
5. Read the story aloud.
6. As you read, invite the children to refine their predictions about the story. Correct the ideas you have previously recorded on the transparency either during the reading or after the reading.

Sample Mini-Lesson on Fact and Opinion

A fact is something that has been proven scientifically and we all agree on. For example, "the earth revolves around the sun" is a statement of fact. An opinion is something that we don't all agree on; an opinion expresses the speaker's idea or point of view. For example, "from outer space, the earth looks like a dinner plate that was painted blue and green" is an opinion. Even though some of us might agree that the earth looks like such a plate, it is still only an opinion, a point of view. It is not a fact because it has not been proven scientifically; nor is it something we would all agree with.

Selective Reading Variation

Read the first paragraph, a middle paragraph, and an ending paragraph from a story and ask the children to fill in the gaps by speculating about the missing elements of the story.

CALL AND RESPONSE

The bulk of the kind of reading that most children do in school is silent reading. And while silent reading is an essential part of any reading program, exclusive emphasis on it shuts children away from the emotive aspects of language. Most children, when they read silently, read without reference to the dynamic qualities of language. The words that pass through their minds usually do so in a mental monotone. If children fail to see how words in print correspond to the kinds of energetic words they use when they speak (or shout, or scream, or whisper, or laugh), they will usually become disinterested in continuing to want to read silently. The Call and Response technique offers children a way to experience the dynamic qualities of print language, and it does so in a way that promotes active and joyful involvement (Hancock 2000; Johns & VanLeirsburg 1994).

Call and Response Process

1. Choose a text to share with children; poems by children's authors are particularly effective. The goal of the activity is to share the ideas in the poem and to promote a joyful sharing and exchange of language.
2. Read the poem, one line at a time. After you read a line, invite the children to mimic the line you just read. Each time you read a line, however, you must read it with energy and enthusiasm, and you must invite the children to mimic your reading with the same energy and enthusiasm that you displayed.
3. You should also consider adding physical motions to each line you read: for instance, you might change your facial expression, raise or wave your hands, cross your arms, stomp your feet, or change your physical posture where appropriate. Invite the children to do the same.
4. Also consider reading each line from a different emotional perspective: sad, happy, surprised, confused, bored, nervous, etc. Ask the children which emotion fits the line (or the poem) the best.

5. You might also use different vocal tones for each line: hollow, nasal, rough, creaky, whispery, etc. Ask the children which tone is most effective for the poem.

Call and Response Variation

Use Paul Fleischman's book of poems, *Joyful Noise: Poems for Two Voices*. Divide children into two groups and invite them to read the poems aloud from Fleischman's book.

CONCERT READING

If children are to receive the full impact of a text read aloud, they need to be stirred both cognitively and emotionally (Booth 1994). By listening to a story or poem read aloud, children can make cognitive strides when they learn to process information and make inferences. But to internalize the story or poem and to make it a part of their mental schemas, children also need to make emotional connections. For it is the emotional aspect of a story or poem that makes the deepest and most profound impact on listeners. One way to help children make and sustain these important emotional connections is to use the Concert Reading technique. With this technique, we read a story or poem aloud with the aid of appropriate background music: wordless music that matches and supports the mood of the text we are reading. When children listen to a story or poem that is supported by mood-matching music, their emotional experience of and response to the text are both deepened and magnified.

Concert Reading Process

1. Choose a story or poem that has a sustained and clear mood: friendly, serious, distant, angry, cheerful, bitter, cynical, reverential, resentful, warm, cold, remorseful, sad, playful, confused, curious, sarcastic, nostalgic, pleading, assertive, gloomy, etc.

2. Choose wordless music that matches the mood of the text you have chosen. Movie soundtracks offer excellent selections because most tracks are structured around a specific mood. Record labels Windham Hill and Narada also offer good choices; the artists who record for them most often play wordless music that is infused with a rich variety of moods.

3. Practice reading the text with the music playing in the background. Be sure that your rate of reading and the volume and pitch of your voice match the mood of the music. Share the Concert Reading with children.

Concert Reading Variation

Use any waltz or the music of John Philip Sousa as background for tempo when reading rhythmic poetry aloud—poetry that has three or four beats. Place the poem on an overhead transparency and invite the children to read along to the rhythm of the music with you.

Another variation is to have the children read poetry to a rap rhythm. Bring in rap music—without the vocals—and present any poem that has a four-beat structure to each line (Mother Goose rhymes work quite well). As the rap rhythm is playing, lead the students in a choral rap reading of the poem.

CHAPTER FOUR

TEACHING CHILDREN TO READ ALOUD

Strategies That Develop Expressive and Interpretative Reading Skills

Children need a lot of oral reading practice to develop fluency.
—Eugene H. Cramer, "Connecting in the Classroom: Ideas from Teachers"

Good readers . . . grow out of good speakers and reciters.
—Eric Havelock, "The Oral-Literature Equation"

Fluent readers are characterized by the ability to read orally with speed, accuracy, and proper expression. . . . Fluency . . . exerts an important influence on comprehension.
—S. Jay Samuels, "Reading Fluency: Its Development and Assessment"

Encouraging appropriate oral interpretation not only assists students with their expressiveness, but also sharpens their insights into the literature for themselves and their listeners.
—Miriam Martinez, Nancy L. Roser, and Susan Strecker, "'I Never Thought I Could Be a Star': A Reader's Theatre Ticket to Fluency"

When children learn to read aloud expressively, they gain greater control over the process of reading: they see how printed texts work, how print language differs from spoken language, and how print language can be understood, interpreted, expressed, and assimilated.

Children do, however, need guidance and practice if they are going to become fluent and expressive oral readers. The following strategies provide scaffolds and processes that will guide children toward developing powerful oral reading skills.

CHORAL READING

When children read expressively together, they form a natural language alliance where they are freer to take risks and to try out new vocalizations. Because reading aloud with expression is often a daunting and scary task for the individual reader, Choral Reading gives children the opportunity to find the support they need to be more relaxed and more successful (Hadaway, Vardell, & Young 2001). Choral Reading also lets children explore the voice of the text and find new ways to speak words and phrases that unearth subtextual meanings. In addition, their articulation and enunciation will improve (Booth & Moore 1988). Moreover, when children engage in Choral Reading activities, they bind their voices and energies together to create a powerful, language-based experience, one that creates a seamless blending of tone and helps cement the text in their minds and memories. In this way, they make the text their own.

Choral Reading Process No. 1

1. Display a short poem on the overhead. For young children, nursery rhymes and chants work especially well.
2. Ask the children to read the piece aloud with you. You will notice that, most of the time, the reading will be flat and inexpressive.
3. Tell the children that, to really come alive, the oral reading needs more expression (vocal variety skills). Talk about the poem's subject matter, its tone, and any significant poetic structures (repetition, simile, metaphor, etc.).
4. Read the text again (without the children), modeling the application of vocal variety skills.
5. Ask children to read the text with you, using the same skills that you used. Practice this phase three or four times until the children grow comfortable with the reading. It is a good idea, especially with young children, to read the poem again the next day and the day after.
6. Invite children to suggest other ways to vocalize the text; they might also suggest gestures or postures to use when reading.
7. The following poem is a Choral Reading selection. Full of emotion (curiosity, discovery, wonder, fear), movement, and repetition, the poem's structure is well suited for vocal variety.

THE WIND

The wind whirls on quicksilver feet.
It rustles leaves and rattles windows.
It bangs shutters and kicks up dust.
Have you ever seen the wind
as it smears your face with its airy caress
as it bends flowers low and shakes up trees?
Have you seen the wind?
No? No?
But the wind, for sure, has seen you and me.

Choral Reading Process No. 2

1. Distribute a copy of "I Can Bellow Like a Giant!" to children or place a copy of it on an overhead projector.
2. Read it aloud once, emphasizing vocal variation.
3. Use the Call and Response technique, reading one line at a time and inviting the children to imitate your way of reading.

Note: This particular script might best follow a unit on folktales. If it is used in another context, it would be helpful for the teacher to explain the situations and give brief summaries for the stories from which the following lines are taken.

I Can Bellow Like a Giant!

When I lift my chin, I speak like strong iron, "I command you to spin all of this straw into golden thread, if you value your life!"

When I clench my teeth, I speak like a knotted rope, "I am sick and tired of letting down my long hair. Get a ladder!"

When I hold my nose, I speak with a twang, "Life in a pumpkin shell is full of pungent, putrid smells."

When I let my arms hang low, I yammer like a troll, "Da, say, who's that a tramping on my bridge?"

When I stand up straight, I howl like a horn, "What'da you mean the apple was poisoned?"

When I speak with air, I whisper like dust, "How did I know a dragon was sleeping in this cave?"

When I grind my words, I speak like gravel, "Little pig, little pig, let me come in!"

When I hollow my sounds, I moan like the wind, "Beware: the Banshee comes in the dead of night."

When I weep and cry, I speak in sobs, "I've lost (sob) my sheep (sob) and I don't know where to find them (sob, sob, sob)."

When I cackle my voice, I speak like rust, "I'll take those ruby slippers, my dear!"

When my mouth gets lazy, I speak like tar, "Hi . . . Ho . . . Hi . . . Ho . . . . oh . . . never . . . mind . . . I . . . think . . . I'll . . . just . . . take . . . a . . . nap."

When I have a cold in my nose, I speak like a full sponge: "Mirror, mirror, on da wall, who'd da fairest of dem all?"

When I open wide my mouth, I speak like a megaphone: "Make me into a mountain!"

When I narrow my eyes, I speak with a thin voice: "Pssst, hey there, you wanna buy some magic beans?"

When I'm the wolf's delight, I speak with a high-pitched voice and show big eyes: "Why Grandma, what big eyes you have!"

When I'm short but haughty, I speak like a squeaky hinge: "Well, Mistress Queen, do you know my name yet?"

When my face slides down, I speak with a low voice, one from my shoes: "Oh no! Oh my! Mighty Casey has struck ooooooout!"

READING "WRONG"

A variation of Choral Reading, Reading "Wrong" helps children see how important the right use of vocal variety is. Because the way a text is read aloud must match the meanings and emotions implied by the text, it is essential that children understand the correlation of one to the other. By inviting children to read a text with vocal skills that do not match the intended tone or meanings, they will make rapid discoveries about why it is important to use the right vocal skills. When children Read "Wrong" they will also have fun, as they will make a kind of game of the activity. Often by seeing what's wrong with something, we then can see what should be right.

Reading "Wrong" Process

1. Display a short poem on the overhead.
2. Invite the children to read it aloud with you.
3. Invite the children to read the poem again, but this time with a vocal inflection that does not match the tone of the poem. For instance, if the poem has a happy tone, read it aloud with a sad voice (low pitch, slow rate, breaking voice).
4. Ask the children why the way they read the poem docs not match the meaning of the poem.
5. Here's a poem to use for Reading "Wrong." How many different ways can this poem be read "wrong"? Notice that the poem has a quiet, subdued, peaceful, almost reverential tone. Notice, too, how the poem changes when it is read with a voice that is loud, strident, or harsh.

TWILIGHT

Beside a hill, my hill, I stood.
    It was sleek with new-laid snow,
Above it the moon hung high
And sent a shivering evening glow.

Silence and silver snow was
    All that I could see—
I stood and watched the cold cold moon
    While it watched me.

GROUP AND SOLO READING

To help children develop a sense of timing, teamwork, and meaning, use the Group and Solo Reading activity (Hadaway, Vardell, & Young 2001). When a reading is preformed by children in groups, they learn the importance of timing: as one group finishes a section, the next group must begin reading without a noticeable pause. When solo parts are added, children must learn teamwork: for group and solo readings to blend, the entire group must work together to create a seamless reading. Finally, children learn to make meaning—how ideas and emotions spring to life via the concert of voices—from the text through their shared experience of performing it.

Group and Solo Reading Process

1. Display a poem on the overhead projector.
2. Divide the children into two groups: A and B.
3. Depending on the length of the poem, ask for some children to volunteer to read solo lines (anywhere from two to eight solo parts may be assigned).
4. Divide the poem so that Group A reads some lines, Group B reads some, and each soloist reads one or two.
5. Practice the poem. Be sure each group and soloist reads with expression and leaves no gaps between lines. This part of the process will take repeated rehearsals so that the groups and soloists can read their lines with energy and expression and so that the lines can be coordinated without noticeable gaps.
6. Here's a text specifically designed for two groups and eight soloists. As you can see, the text is comprised of Mother Goose rhymes and elaborations based on the rhymes' content and ideas.

MOTHER GOOSE AND MORE!

Group A:	Humpty Dumpty sat on the wall Humpty Dumpty had a great fall.
Group B:	All the king's horses and all the king's men Couldn't put Humpty together again.
Group A:	Jack be nimble, Jack be quick,
Group B:	Jack jump over the candle stick.
Soloist 1:	Humpty Dumpty crashed down to the ground,
Soloist 2:	And Jack jumped over him in a single bound!
Group A:	Dickery, dickery dare, The pig flew up in the air;
Group B:	The man in brown Soon brought him down, Dickery, dickery, dare.
Group A:	Old Mother Goose, When she wanted to wander,
Group B:	Would ride through the air On a very fine gander.
Soloist 3:	When Old Mother Goose flew through the air
Soloist 4:	She crashed into a flying pig up there!

Soloist 5:	The man dressed in brown
Soloist 6:	Brought Mother Goose down,
Soloist 7:	And the pig came tumbling after.
Group A:	There was a crooked man,
	And he walked a crooked mile,
	He found a crooked sixpence
	Against a crooked stile;
Group B:	He bought a crooked cat,
	Which caught a crooked mouse,
	And they all lived together
	In a little crooked house.
Soloist 8:	But when the crooked man
Soloist 1:	Slept in his crooked bed
Soloist 2:	He had crooked dreams
Soloist 3:	Inside his crooked head!
Group A:	Jack Sprat could eat no fat,
	His wife could eat no lean,
	And so between them both, you see,
	They licked the platter clean.
Group B:	Ladies and gentlemen, come to supper—
	We have hot boiled beans and very good butter!
Group A:	Jack would eat no butter;
Group B:	His wife would eat no beans,
Soloist 4:	And so, between them both, you see,
Soloist 5:	They stayed quite thin and lean!
Group A:	A wise old owl sat in an oak,
	The more he heard
Group B:	the less he spoke.
Group A:	The less he spoke
Group B:	the more he heard.
Groups A & B:	Why aren't we all like that wise old bird!?

BUDDY READING

To provide children with immediate support and positive feedback, invite them to participate in the Buddy Reading activity. Buddy Reading also helps struggling readers make gains in word recognition, fluency, and comprehension (Richards 2000). In this activity, a child who may be struggling with reading works with a reading buddy—someone who is more proficient at reading. The reading buddy may be an adult (parent, grandparent, teacher, etc.), an older child, or a peer. The two sit together and both read aloud a text they have agreed upon. As they read, the reading buddy points to the words on the page. If the struggling reader hesitates or stumbles, the reading buddy can gently offer assistance or ask questions that might lead the struggling reader to figure out how to make the necessary reading adjustments.

Buddy Reading Process

1. Both readers meet to read an agreed-upon text.
2. Both begin reading aloud. The initial reading should probably take from five to ten minutes. The time can be increased with additional meetings.
3. If the struggling reader wants to read solo, he or she lets the buddy know.
4. If the struggling reader stumbles, he or she can either self-correct or receive help from the buddy.

INDIVIDUAL READING

At some point, we will want most, if not all, children to read aloud individually. Individual Reading is a perfect way for children to share what they have been reading on their own. When children read aloud a section of self-selected text (after repeated practice with vocal variety skills), they are engaging in an authentic way of sharing the books they enjoy (Martinez, Roser, & Strecker 1999). Children can also read selections from a genre study. If, for example, children are studying poetry, each child might choose to read aloud a favorite poem. When children read aloud individually, they will demonstrate their understandings and interpretations of printed texts.

Individual Reading Process

1. Read aloud to children. By doing so, you will serve as a strong model of proficient, expressive reading.
2. Remind them, as you are reading, to listen to how you use vocal variety. Point to the Oral Reading Reminder chart if you have one (see pages 21 and 22).
3. Invite children to select a text or part of a text to read aloud. Tell them that their reading should last between two to four minutes. Give them ample time to make vocal variety notations in the text and to practice. Also give them time to meet in Reading Response Groups to get constructive feedback from their peers.
4. Allow children to sign up for readings on the days and times that they would like.
5. At the allotted times, children read aloud their selections.

READ IT AGAIN

The Read It Again activity helps children realize the importance of vocal variety in the creation, delivery of meaning, and the importance of repeated oral readings (Samuels 2002). Because they are reading minimal texts—texts with little context—they need to use their voices (and gestures) to help listeners gain a sense of the scene that is being created. As children read, they will have to form clear mental images of who they are in the scene, why they are there, and what they mean to communicate. When children participate in Read It Again, they learn to use the words as springboards into the place where image, context, and intention unite to furnish meaning.

Process for Read It Again

1. Divide children into pairs.
2. Give each pair a minimal text.
3. Ask them to read it aloud together in such a way that lets the listeners know how each reader feels. Each pair should practice the text before reading it in front of the group. Remind them to use the skills of vocal variety.
4. Invite one pair of students to read.
5. After they have read, ask the listeners to describe how each reader was feeling.
6. Ask the readers to verify or deny the listeners' assertions.
7. Ask another pair to read the text again, but to read it differently, to express different emotions.
8. Here are three minimal texts:

DIALOGUE NO. 1

Person A:	hello	Person B:	hello
Person A:	how are you?	Person B:	okay
Person A:	great	Person B:	yeah
Person A:	okay	Person B:	I see
Person A:	sure	Person B:	bye

DIALOGUE NO. 2

Person A:	ready	Person B:	now
Person A:	yeah	Person B:	sure
Person A:	okay	Person B:	now
Person A:	now	Person B:	let's go
Person A:	go	Person B:	okay

DIALOGUE NO. 3

Person A:	you	Person B:	me
Person A:	yes	Person B:	it's me
Person A:	yes	Person B:	right
Person A:	yes	Person B:	yeah
Person A:	terrific	Person B:	well

READER'S THEATRE

When children perform a Reader's Theatre script, they must muster all of their vocal talents and plumb their interpretative imaginations to deliver a story or a poem to listeners. Performing a Reader's Theatre also enables children to take full advantage of the vocal variety skills they have been working on. When children take part in a Reader's Theatre, they do not have to memorize lines; concern themselves with props or blocking; or worry about sets, lighting, or costumes. They stand in front of an audience and read their scripts, relying on their voices, postures, and gestures to communicate the message of the text (Hancock 2000; Davis 1997).

Reader's Theatre Process

Select a text to turn into a Reader's Theatre script. *Aesop's Fables* work very well. Use the guidelines below to divide the text into parts: narrators and characters.

Guidelines for Turning a Story into a Reader's Theatre Script.   Most stories have uneven parts for a narrator and the characters. To even the reading parts, follow the directions below. The resulting script will be one that contains roughly the same amount for every performer to read.

1. Every important character will have a narrator (an alter ego).
2. Minor characters may be read by one person and still have one narrator. (Remember: Every sentence has object and action—subject and predicate. The narrator will usually read the part of the sentence that introduces the action; the characters will read the action part of the sentences.)
3. Narrators read ONLY those parts of a sentence that include THE NAME of their characters and PRONOUNS that refer to their characters.
4. Characters read passages that depict their actions. Characters MAY NEVER read passages that include their names or pronouns that refer to them.
5. The prose piece should be broken up EVENLY; every person should have approximately the same amount to read.
6. No words in the text may be changed or eliminated.
7. Words and phrases can be added if they are ones uttered by the characters.

Next, assign parts or let the children choose parts. Rehearse the script. Use vocal variety, posture, and gesture to communicate the actions and reactions. Perform and enjoy!

Here is an example of a traditional text, one of *Aesop's Fables:*

THE WOLF AND THE CRANE: ORIGINAL VERSION

A wolf once got a bone stuck in his throat. Trying to dislodge the bone, he began rolling on the ground. But the bone remained stuck as a rusty key in an old lock. He grew so desperate that he even stuck his head in the stream to try and wash out the bone, but still the bone remained stuck. Finally, the wolf loped over to a crane and begged her to put her long bill into his throat and pull out the bone. "I'll reward you," rasped the wolf. The crane hesitated for a moment and then did as he asked. With a click and a clack, the crane easily pulled the bone out of the wolf's throat. The wolf thanked her warmly and turned away when the crane cried, "What about my reward?" "Reward indeed!" snapped the wolf, baring his teeth as he spoke. "You can go boasting that you once put your head into a wolf's mouth and didn't get it bitten off. What more do you want?" So the wolf got what he wanted and the crane was cheated out of her reward.

Moral: The weak cannot demand justice from the strong.

If we were to turn this text into a traditional Reader's Theatre script, this is how it would look. Notice how uneven the parts are; the narrator gets to read the bulk of the story:

THE WOLF AND THE CRANE: TRADITIONAL (UNBALANCED) READER THEATRE'S SCRIPT

Narrator: A wolf once got a bone stuck in his throat. Trying to dislodge the bone, he began rolling on the ground. But the bone remained stuck as a rusty key in an old lock. He grew so desperate that he even stuck his head in the stream to try and wash out the bone, but still the bone remained stuck. Finally, the wolf loped over to a crane and begged her to put her long bill into his throat and pull out the bone.

Wolf: "I'll reward you,"

Narrator: rasped the wolf. The crane hesitated for a moment and then did as he asked. With a click and a clack, the crane easily pulled the bone out of the wolf's throat. The wolf thanked her warmly and turned away when the crane cried,

Crane: "What about my reward?"

Wolf: "Reward indeed!"

Narrator: snapped the wolf, baring his teeth as he spoke.

Wolf: "You can go boasting that you once put your head into a wolf's mouth and didn't get it bitten off. What more do you want?"

Narrator: So the wolf got what he wanted and the crane was cheated out of her reward.

Moral: *The weak cannot demand justice from the strong.*

If we apply the guidelines for turning a story into a Reader's Theatre script, we arrive at a much more balanced text, one where both narrators and both characters have about the same amount to read:

THE WOLF AND THE CRANE: A BALANCED READER'S THEATRE SCRIPT

Parts: *Two Narrators, Wolf, Crane*

Note: Wolf and Crane should read their lines with appropriate intonation and inflection.

N 1: A wolf once got a bone stuck in his throat. Trying to dislodge the bone, he began

Wolf: rolling on the ground. But the bone remained stuck as a rusty key in an old lock.

N 1: He grew so desperate that he even stuck his head

Wolf:	in the stream to try and wash out the bone, but still the bone remained stuck.
N 1:	Finally, the wolf
Wolf:	loped over to a crane and begged her to put her long bill
N 1:	into his throat and pull out the bone.
Wolf:	"I'll reward you,"
N 1:	rasped the wolf.
N 2:	The crane hesitated for a moment
Crane:	and then did as he asked.
N 2:	With a click and a clack, the crane
Crane:	easily pulled the bone out of the wolf's throat.
N 1:	The wolf
Wolf:	thanked her warmly and turned away
N 2:	when the crane cried,
Crane:	"What about my reward?"
Wolf:	"Reward indeed!"
N 1:	snapped the wolf, baring his teeth as he spoke.
Wolf:	"You can go boasting that you once put your head into a wolf's mouth and didn't get it bitten off. What more do you want?"
N 1:	So the wolf got what he wanted
N 2:	and the crane was cheated out of her reward.
N 2:	Moral:
Crane:	The weak cannot demand justice
Wolf:	from the strong.

We can also "jazz up" the script by adding vocal elaborations—other things that the characters could say (the elaborations are in parentheses):

THE WOLF AND THE CRANE: A BALANCED SCRIPT WITH VOCAL ELABORATIONS

Parts:	*Two Narrators, Wolf, Crane*
Note:	Wolf and Crane should read their lines with appropriate intonation and inflection.
N 1:	A wolf once got a bone stuck in his throat.
Wolf:	(Ahhhh! No more spicy chicken wings for me!)
N 1:	Trying to dislodge the bone, he began
Wolf:	rolling on the ground. But the bone remained as stuck as a rusty key in an old lock.
N 1:	He grew so desperate

Wolf: (Maybe if I gargled with a little river water)

N 1: that he even stuck his head

Wolf: in the stream to try and wash out the bone, but still the bone remained stuck.

N 1: Finally, the wolf

Wolf: loped over to a crane and begged her to put her long bill

N 1: into his throat and pull out the bone.

Wolf: "I'll reward you,"

N 1: rasped the wolf.

N 2: The crane hesitated for a moment

Crane: and then did as he asked.

N 2: With a click and a clack, the crane

Crane: easily pulled the bone out of the wolf's throat (Oh, my. He could certainly use a bottle of mouthwash.)

N 1: The wolf thanked her warmly

Wolf: (Oh, you must come over for dinner sometime . . .)

N 1: and turned away.

N 2: When the crane cried,

Crane: "What about my reward?"

Wolf: "Reward indeed!"

N 1: snapped the wolf, baring his teeth as he spoke.

Wolf: "You can go boasting that you once put your head into a wolf's mouth and didn't get it bitten off. What more do you want?"

N 1: So the wolf got what he wanted

N 2: and the crane was cheated out of her reward.

N 2: Moral:

Crane: The weak cannot demand justice

Wolf: from the strong.

CHAPTER FIVE

WRITING TO READ ALOUD

Reasons and Ways to Write
for the Expressive Voice

*As part of their understanding of the symbolic features of written language,
children also need to become aware that there is a relationship
between print and speech or between talk and writing.*
—Liliana Barro Zecker, "Different Texts, Different Emergent Writing Forms"

*Good writers are good readers . . . and better
readers tend to produce better writing.*
—Marci S. Popp, *Teaching Language and Literature in Elementary Classrooms*

Writing is best learned in conjunction with meaningful reading activities.
—Diane Kern, Wendy Andre, Rebecca Schilke, James Barton, and Margaret Conn
McGuire, "Less Is More: Preparing Students for State Writing Assessments"

*Effective writers hear what they are saying as they say it and actually
pace and tune their sentences between the moment they
are heard and [when] the words appear on the screen.*
—Donald M. Murray, *Crafting a Life: In Essay, Story, Poem*

While it is essential that children become immersed in literature by actively listening to daily
read-alouds and by learning how to read aloud expressively, it is also important that children
learn to write their own texts—ones that they will, in turn, use as read-aloud vehicles. Reading
and writing are two ways of working with words that are mutually supportive and intimately
connected. The more children read, the better they write. And the more children write, the
better they read. As children are exposed to a wealth of quality literature (especially when they
use expressive skills to read that literature aloud), they will discover powerful models to emulate for their own writing (Hancock 2000).

As they work through the writing process to emulate these models, children also need
many occasions to read their works aloud (Bishop 1998). When students read their works

aloud in the Writing Response Groups, they have a chance to hear how their work sounds and to get feedback in a safe environment. After they have shared their work with their peers and have revised it sufficiently, they can then meet in Reading Response Groups to prepare to read their work to a larger audience.

REASONS TO WRITE FOR THE EXPRESSIVE VOICE

1. *To link reading, writing, speaking, and listening.* For children to achieve high levels of literacy, they must have frequent occasions to integrate all aspects of the language arts: reading, writing, speaking, and listening. By integrating these aspects of the language arts, children will discover a holistic and potent way to make sense of their experiences and to learn new skills and concepts (Au, Carroll, & Scheu 2001; Popp 1996). As children create texts to read aloud, they will learn new writing skills (invention, organization, development, word choice); they will also use critical reading skills to evaluate how well they have written, and they must listen effectively to the members of their peer response groups as they get feedback about the texts they have constructed. Additionally, when children write to read aloud, they will use language that promotes thought (generating, organizing, and developing ideas; critical analysis of self-generated texts for the purposes of revision and oral expression), which, in turn, promotes a better understanding of language (Kelso 2000; Vygotsky 1962).

2. *To become sensitive to the ways that words and genres express meaning.* When children actively listen to texts read aloud with an ear toward discovering rich language (as described in Chapter 1), they will, in turn, be more sensitive to the kinds of rich words they can use in their own writing (Kern, Andre, Schilke, Barton, & McGuire 2003). Because they have been exposed to so much rich language in the texts they have heard and read aloud, their horizons of word choice expand and they discover new ways to articulate thoughts, ideas, and perceptions. Additionally, through their experiences with spoken texts, children will also realize new rhetorical and structural choices. Because they have heard, and have read aloud, a variety of stories, poems, and works of nonfiction, children will see that these texts are all organized differently and that the variety of organizational structures express different ideas. These texts, then, become the prior knowledge that children need to be able to transfer text structures, concepts, and words from one context to another—from the texts that others have written to the texts that the children will create. By examining and modeling the text structures of professional authors, children will learn new ways to organize, develop, and convey personal experiences, observations, and discoveries (Ray 1999; Zecker 1999; Moore 1995). In this way, their writings will be more firmly focused and more tightly bound; and there is a much stronger chance that those writings will avoid being a random collection of phrases and sentences.

3. *To understand the importance of audience.* When children write to read aloud, they will come to see that audience plays a key role in determining what they will write and how much effort they will put into the act of writing. Traditionally and generally, children write for one audience: the teacher. And when the teacher is the only audience, children often have a hard time understanding the importance of writing for different audiences. But when they know that the audience will be their peers, they will be more interested in selecting genres and registers (use and tone of words) that are appropriate for their listeners (Smith 1994). In other words, they will learn that an awareness of audience helps them decide what to say and how to say it.

4. *To establish clear purposes.* When children become aware of the importance of audience, they will also understand the importance of choosing clear purposes for their writing. Often children write with one purpose in mind: to complete an assignment. When they are writing for an audience of their peers (or for other audiences, e.g., parents or students in other classes), they will see that the purpose of their writing—whether it be to inform, persuade, describe, delight, or define—must be fully realized and articulated. They will also see that, through direct instruction, they must choose the best genres to carry the freight of their purposes and ideas (Ray 1999; Moore 1995).

5. *To develop voice.* All children have something important to say. Many children, however, don't know how to say it as powerfully and as clearly as they would like. Many children get stumped when it comes to developing their own strong writing voice. And beginning or struggling writers usually see that their writing voice is nowhere nearly as sharp and crisp as the voices in the texts they are using as writing models (Furr 2003).

To help children develop strong voices we should teach them this maxim: voice = choice. Which is to say that voice in writing is a combination of two things: choice of words and choice of sentence length. A writer's voice is expressed through his or her choice of words (concrete or abstract, general or specific, plain or figurative) and sentence length (simple, compound, complex, or compound-complex). Notice, for example, the different voices in the following three sentences:

   a. The room was a mess.
   b. Boxes, bespeckled and with rose-tinted stipples of paint, were strewn throughout the white-walled chamber.
   c. Scarred floorboards groaned beneath the dead weight of the sagging walls; shattered windows, like fractured eyes, stared inward at the wreck of the room, filtering the sun into splinters of sour light.

The first sentence has a vague voice because the sentence is short and simple; the words are general, nonspecific. No details are given. The second sentence has stronger voice, though it is more formal. The words *bespeckled, rose-tinted, stipples, strewn,* and *chamber* give the sentence a formal voice; these words are usually not used in everyday conversation. The third sentence has a more somber, ornate voice. The sentence is longer and the words are more detailed and richly textured. Notice the use of strong adjectives, metaphor, and simile; these are what lends the voice its somber, baroque quality.

To help children develop a strong voice in their writing, we need to help them make effective choices (Kern, Andre, Schilke, Barton, & McGuire 2003). By using literature as a model for their writing, we can show children how professional authors have chosen words and sentences to create voice. As children learn to see the choices authors have made, they are in a much stronger position to make their own choices about words and sentences.

When we provide children with a strong foundation in oral literacy, we are giving them one of the strongest means possible for transferring that oral foundation into a dynamic written one (Kelso 2000). Because, in an oral reading program, children analyze texts to read aloud, they develop a stronger understanding of how professional authors use words and sentences to

■ ■ ■ ■ ■

REASONS TO WRITE FOR THE EXPRESSIVE VOICE

1. To link reading, writing, speaking, and listening.
2. To become sensitive to the ways that words and genres express meaning.
3. To understand the importance of audience.
4. To establish clear purposes.
5. To develop voice.
6. To help second language learners gain greater control over English.
7. To address national legislation.

communicate ideas and emotions. Additionally, as children develop their reading voices, so too will they be able to integrate that knowledge into their writing.

6. *To help second language learners gain greater control over English.* When children, whose first language is not English, are guided through clearly focused writing activities, they are able to transfer words, concepts, and text structures from one language to another (Barrett-Pugh & Rohl 2001). When children have parallel development in two languages, they are able to express their thoughts and ideas in meaningful ways. When guided through writing activities, children are also able to develop a stronger awareness of the nature of language and how language works. And when children are given the opportunity to read aloud, in an expressive way, the work they have written, they make further progress in developing the metalinguistic awareness they need to gain greater control over a second language.

7. *To address national legislation.* With the passing of the No Child Left Behind legislation, we need to give children repeated interactions with all aspects of language (Au, Carroll, & Scheu 2001; Popp 1996). If we want to make sure that all children have every chance to succeed, we need to help them learn to integrate language so that they can read, write, speak, and listen in ways that are dynamic, proactive, interactive, enjoyable, and meaningful. Writing to read aloud will help all children make just the kinds of gains they need to make so that none of them are left behind.

LITERATURE-BASED WRITING: A Springboard to Read-Aloud Scripts

While quality literature provides children with texts to read aloud, it also provides them with structures and patterns that can help them organize their thoughts so they can write about and come to make sense of their experiences both at home and in the classroom (Ray 1999; Moore 1995). And the texts that children create also need to be shared, via oral reading, with their mentors and peers. When children gather together to read aloud the texts they have written, an authentic community of readers and writers is established at the ground level—at the level of the lived experiences of the children (McCracken & McCracken 1998; Coody 1997).

One of the problems that many children face when they write, however, is that they do not know what choices they have, or could have, as writers (Noden 1999; Bishop 1998;

Hillocks 1995; Hunt 1993). They often know neither the variety of writing patterns, forms, and structures that are available to them, nor the methods of actively creating meaning by using those forms. In other words, children are often limited in their writing because they do not know that all types of writing are governed by clear and specific structural elements and that the most effective writing is most often done in a recursive process.

To assist children in becoming acquainted with writerly choices, we can furnish them with literature-based models to emulate and a recursive process to follow (Smith 1994; Stewig 1980). By yoking quality books and the writing process—models and methods—we can give children the tools and procedures they need to create lively, thought-filled texts—texts they create for, and read to, specific audiences.

The literature-based, process writing activities in this chapter are designed to help young writers enjoy writing success. These activities, all of which have been thoroughly classroom tested, are grounded in the premises that reading and writing are mutually supportive, symbiotic activities, and that when children learn to see writing as process-oriented, they will discover new and exciting ways to create texts that they can share aloud.

Often when we ask children to compose a piece of writing, they ask in return, "How long should it be?" When children ask this question, we know that they are struggling and that their writing will not be very effective; most likely, it will be underdeveloped and disorganized (Collins 1998). Successful writers think about writing by asking themselves these questions: What form of writing should I use (an expository paragraph, a descriptive paragraph, a blank verse poem, a ballad, an editorial, a riddle, an essay, a research paper, etc.)? And how should I structure that form so that I can help my audience best understand the ideas I am trying to communicate?

If we want to enable children to write successfully, we need to move them away from thinking solely about length. Instead we want to teach them to choose the best forms that will enable their audience to understand the ideas they are hoping to convey (Buss & Karnowski 2000; Ray 1999; Zecker 1999; Cope & Kalantzis 1993; Berthoff 1981). In other words, we want to teach children to write toward, and for, an audience; to pick the forms (and to understand how to construct those forms) that most effectively convey their ideas; and to revise those forms so that the audience can understand what the writers are trying to communicate (Langer & Applebee 1987).

THE WRITING PROCESS: Procedures to Produce Products to Read Aloud

The activities in this chapter focus on some of the forms that children need to learn to use to become stronger writers. They are designed to be starting points: these guided writing activities guide children toward the creation of clearly defined texts. Many beginning and struggling writers benefit greatly from explicit instruction in how to write (Furr 2003). As such, the activities in this chapter will help children learn how to make a variety of important choices at each stage of the writing process. Once children gain a sense of how the writing process works and create a variety of texts via explicit instruction, we encourage them to move to the writing workshop where they pick the topic, form, and purpose of their own writing.

The activities show the writing process in action; they offer a step-by-step approach to teaching children how to create different forms based on pieces of quality literature—forms that many children do not understand and consequently cannot control in their attempts to write them.

As such, these activities call for a slowing down of the teaching of writing so that children can take their time to successfully and thoughtfully move through each step. It is important, though, to recognize that the prewriting stage is usually the most important step of the writing process, and that writers should spend something like 70 percent of their time at this stage. This point cannot be stressed too much.

Each activity is based on a particular children's book and is divided into five parts: prewriting, drafting, revising, editing, and sharing/publishing. Because each of these stages is an essential component of the writing process, each one should be fully and completely implemented.

While it will be very helpful—and strongly suggested!—to have the corresponding children's book for each of these activities, it is not essential because each activity contains clear examples of what the children are being asked to write.

It would also be a good idea if the writing-guide—that is, an adult or a teacher—joins the children when they write and creates his or her own examples of the activities in this chapter. In this way, the writing-guide can come to an experiential understanding of what the children are doing, what problems they might encounter, and ways to help them solve those problems.

The easiest way to use these activities is to follow the directions in the order they are given. During the prewriting stage of each activity the writing-guide should have a conversation with the children—especially when brainstorming—and write the children's prewriting ideas and brainstorming lists on a blackboard or on an overhead transparency. Such written lists will serve as reference points and as idea-stimulators as the children begin to draft.

The drafting stage of each activity allows the writing-guide to show his or her children the various forms they are writing and also to teach mini-lessons on various grammatical structures that children can use (some are already built into some of the lessons).

During the revising and editing stage of each activity, the writing-guide should invite the children to work in groups and to use the directions for these stages as rubrics against which the students can check their own work and the work of their partners. As the children move into these stages, the children might want to consult the Writer's Tools (pages 99–103) to see if they can add any of the elements they find there. The writing-guide might also want to work with groups of children or with individuals as they revise. His or her suggestions and examples will be very helpful.

Once children have prewritten, drafted, revised, and edited, they should share their work with one another, either in small or large groups. The sharing is the key to creating a community of readers and writers. And children will share their writings most effectively if they do not read their writings "cold," but practice by using the skills of vocal variety. As children share their writings aloud, they will become part of a lively, oral community of readers and writers. By becoming part of such a community, children will also have a stronger investment in creating their texts because they know they will be sharing them with their peers. Also, children will be more interested in effectively reading what they have written because they know they will have a live and engaged audience. When children become part of such a community, they find authentic reasons to read, write, and share.

The activities can be modified for children with different developmental and/or writing abilities. For young children, the writing-guide can simplify the activities by reducing sentence length, the structure of the forms, or the kinds of figurative language the children might use.

FIVE RECURSIVE STEPS IN THE WRITING PROCESS

1. PREWRITING: Seventy percent of a writer's time should be spent generating ideas for writing. At this stage, writers should consider: subject, audience, purpose, form, and specific ways to generate and organize ideas. Prewriting strategies include (but are not limited to): reading aloud, brainstorming, clustering, freewriting, conversing, questioning, daydreaming, imaging, wondering, arguing, webbing, rewriting other works, sharing words, telling jokes, finding rhymes, looking at homophones, creating similes and metaphors, and playing with language patterns.

2. DRAFTING: After rehearsing ideas, writers should choose the best forms for their writing and begin constructing them: they should take their best ideas from the prewriting stage and move them into the forms they have chosen. At this stage, writers should not edit, that is, they should not be overly concerned with mechanical matters.

3. REVISING: Writers look at their work (and ask someone else to) and try to reimagine it, that is, to see it from a new point of view to find new ideas and/or better ways of expressing the ideas in the writing. (Writers might use more rehearsing strategies at this point.) At this stage, mini-lessons can be introduced: grammar and usage items, patterns and structures. See the Writer's Tools pages.

4. EDITING (attending to syntactic, stylistic, and/or mechanical matters): Writers "clean up" their writing by making sure that it is free from syntactic, grammatical, usage, spelling, and punctuation errors. This is often a tedious and difficult stage, but it is absolutely essential.

5. SHARING/PUBLISHING: Once the work has been edited, it should be read aloud.

PATTERNS

AN ALLITERATIVE SENTENCE SLOTTING ACTIVITY

USING MARY ELTING'S Q IS FOR DUCK
AS THE BASIS FOR AN ALLITERATIVE SENTENCE

Purpose: To create an alliterative sentence and respond to literature with a divergent product

Summary: *Q Is for Duck* (Clarion 1980) is a guessing game for young readers. It presents a repeating sentence pattern about animals in the form of a question.

BEFORE WRITING: READING TO WRITE

Read *Q Is for Duck* by Mary Elting and pay special attention to the pattern in the book: _____ is for _____ because _____.

EXAMPLES:

A is for Zoo because animals live there.
B is for Dog because it barks (or is a beagle, or likes bones, or has bad breath).

STEP ONE: PREWRITING

Topic: A fairy tale character or an object

Audience: Other class members

Form: An alliterative sentence

Purposes: To inform, to use alliteration

Generate and Organize Ideas

   a. List characters or objects from fairy tales (or stories you have read).

   EXAMPLES:

   Rapunzel, Magic Harp, Big Bad Wolf, Cinderella, Snow White, Giant Apple, Rumplestiltskin, Troll

   b. Choose a character (e.g., Rapunzel) or object and then list letters from the alphabet that do not begin with the character's (or object's) name.

   EXAMPLES:

   A   G   L   Q   T

   c. List words that begin with that letter, words that might also pertain to the character or object (consulting a dictionary may be helpful).

   EXAMPLES: "L" WORDS FOR RAPUNZEL

lonely	loveless	locked
lived	lost	lass
left	law	land
little	language	long-suffering
languish	low	location

STEP TWO: DRAFTING

Use this sentence slotting pattern to write an alliterative sentence about the character or object you have chosen:

_____ is for _____ because _____.

Definition: Alliteration

Alliteration refers to the repetition of the same consonant sound or of different vowel sounds at the beginning of a series of words or stressed syllables.

EXAMPLES:

Peter Piper picked a peck of pickled peppers.
She sells seashells at the seashore.

Guidelines for Writing an Alliterative Sentence Using the *Q Is for Duck* Pattern

   a. In the first blank place a letter.

   b. In the second blank place the name of the character (or object) that does not begin with the letter in the first blank.

c. In the third blank give an explanation, which may be words, a phrase, or a sentence; the explanation must contain words that begin with the letter in the first blank and must also contain "correct" information about the character. The explanation may, however, be divergent.

EXAMPLE:

L is for Rapunzel because she lived a lonely life.

STEP THREE: REVISING

- Delete weak verbs, adverbs, and adjectives; replace them with stronger ones.
- Strive to create a sentence that vividly and imaginatively describes your character.
- The sentence should also offer correct information about the character.

EXAMPLE (THE ERRORS ARE INTENTIONAL):

L is for Rapunzelll because she was an luckles and a unloved lasss that was left alone to languish in her tower, she lived a lonely long-locked life.

STEP FOUR: EDITING

- Is the sentence a complete sentence and not a run-on or a fragment?
- Are pronouns used correctly?
- Are words spelled correctly?
- Is proper punctuation used: commas, semi-colons, apostrophes?

EXAMPLE:

L is for Rapunzel because she was a luckless and unloved lass who was left alone to languish in her tower where she lived a lonely, long-locked life.

STEP FIVE: SHARING/PUBLISHING

Read your sentence aloud.

AN INTERROGATIVE SENTENCE SLOTTING ACTIVITY

USING JOHN BURNINGHAM'S WOUND YOU RATHER . . .
TO GENERATE A DIVERGENT, INTERROGATIVE SENTENCE

Purposes: To create questions, offer choices, use parallel construction, and use prepositional phrases as a sentence expansion technique

Summary: *Would You Rather* . . . (HarperTrophy 1987) offers young readers a series of "silly" choices in the form of questions. Each question begins with the words "Would you rather . . ."

BEFORE WRITING: READING TO WRITE

a. What do you think the title means?

b. Make five predictions as to what you think this book will be about. Do not worry about "being right"!

c. As you read *Would You Rather* . . . , think about the questions that are asked and how you would answer them.

STEP ONE: PREWRITING

Topic: Animals, objects, events

Audience: Other class members

Form: An interrogative sentence (question)

Purposes: To question, offer choices, use parallel construction, and use prepositional phrases as a sentence expansion technique

Generate and Organize Ideas

   a. Make a list of objects and animals (nouns) such as trees, spoons, cake, shoes, car, umbrella, zebra, python, monkey, elephant, mouse, wolf, leopard . . .

   b. Make a list of action verbs (these do not need to be related to animals) such as share, chase, run, tag, play, climb, hide, race, eat, hug, ride, discover . . .

STAGE TWO: DRAFTING

Definition: Interrogative Sentence

An interrogative sentence is a sentence that asks a question; it ends with a question mark.

Guidelines for Writing a "Would You Rather" Interrogative Sentence

   a. Choose two animals or two objects: for example, wolf and mouse.

   b. Choose two action verbs: for example, race and chase (the verbs can be related, but they don't have to be).

   c. Combine them into a question that begins with the words "would you rather" and follows this pattern (one that offers at least two choices):

Would you rather _____ a _____ or _____ a _____ ?

EXAMPLE:

Would you rather be racing a wolf or chasing a mouse?

STAGE THREE: REVISING

   a. Add prepositional phrases to the question; make a list of prepositions.

Definition: Preposition

A preposition is a word that shows the relationship of a noun or pronoun to another word.

EXAMPLES OF PREPOSITIONS:

in, on, beneath, below, beside, among, along, before, under, with, of, to, for, by, from, toward, at, against, after, until, beyond, during, near, atop, above, through, across . . .

   b. Change the verb tense if you want to.

EXAMPLE:

Would you rather race a growling wolf through a tangled forest or chase a squeaking mouse across your backyard?

c. If you want to, you can make the sentence outrageous by adding strange details.

EXAMPLE:

Would you rather race a growling wolf soaring in a blue hot air balloon or chasing a mouse riding on a yellow motorcycle?

STAGE FOUR: EDITING

a. Be sure the question is parallel—both groups of words on each side of the word "or" must be structured the same way.

b. Be sure the question ends with a question mark.

EXAMPLE:

Would you rather race a growling wolf soaring in a blue hot air balloon or chase a murmuring mouse riding on a yellow motorcycle?

STAGE FIVE: PUBLISHING

Read your questions aloud or compile a class book of "would you rather . . ." questions.

A RESEARCH PATTERN POEM

USING CHRISTINE BUTTERWORTH'S FROGS *TO WRITE A RESEARCH POEM*

Objectives: To read and think critically and to report findings in ways that require synthesis

Summary: *Frogs* (Raintree Steck-Vaughn 1990) offers information about the nature of frogs.

BEFORE READING: READING TO WRITE

Make a list of everything you know about frogs, and everything you think you know (guessing is encouraged).

What I Know   What I Think I Know

STEP ONE: PREWRITING

Topic: Frogs

Audience: Other students

Form: A listing model

Purpose: To report research

Generate and Organize Ideas

After reading about frogs, place information beneath the following headings:

DATABASE

Colors	Activities	Homes	Sounds	Attributes
green	jump	ponds	croak	big eyes
blue	catch flies	rivers	peep	smooth skin

STEP TWO: DRAFTING

Use the information you have gathered in the following model:

I am frog, come to my home in _____

I am frog, hear me _____

I am frog, see my _____

I am frog, watch me _____

I am frog, hear me, see me, but watch out, I may be watching you!

EXAMPLE:

I am frog, come to my home
in ponds, lakes, rivers, and deserts.
I am frog, hear me
croak.
I am frog, see my
smooth skin,
my big eyes,
webbed feet,
my fingers.
I am frog, watch me
jumping,
swim underwater,
catch a fly,
and puffed up my chin.
I am frog, hear me, see me, but watch out, I may be watching you!

STEP THREE: REVISING

Check your report and see if you can add describing words.

EXAMPLE:

I am frog, come to my home
in ponds, lakes, rivers, and deserts.
I am frog, hear me
croak and plop.
I am frog, see my
smooth spotted skin,
my big bumpy eyes,
webbed back feet,
my tiny front fingers.
I am frog, watch me
jumping,
swim underwater,
catch a fly,
and puffed up my chin.
I am frog, hear me, see me, but watch out,
I may be watching you!

STEP FOUR: EDITING

- Check your report and make sure the lines that begin each stanza is capitalized.
- Be sure to end each stanza with a period—or an exclamation point.
- Be sure all the verbs are the same tense.

EXAMPLE:

I am frog, come to my home
in ponds, lakes, rivers, and deserts.
I am frog, hear me
croak and plop.
I am frog, see my
smooth spotted skin,
my big bumpy eyes,
webbed back feet,
my tiny front fingers.
I am frog, watch me
jump from pad to pond,
swim underwater,
catch a fly,
and puff up my chin like a balloon.
I am frog, hear me, see me, but watch out,
I may be watching you!

STEP FIVE: SHARING/PUBLISHING

Read your report aloud.

A CONTRAST PATTERN

USING MARGERY FACKLAM'S THE BIG BUG BOOK *TO CREATE A CONTRAST PATTERN*

Objectives: To read and think critically, see differences, and report findings in ways that require synthesis

Summary: *The Big Bug Book* (Little Brown 1998) by Margery Facklam presents information on a variety of large bugs.

STEP ONE: PREWRITING

Audience: Class members

Form: Contrast pattern/sentence slotting

Purpose: To show differences, use concrete details to support a main idea

Content: Animals/insects

Generate and Organize Ideas

Create databases for two animals. Use these headings; be sure to put at least 5 concrete details beneath each heading.

Attributes	Actions	Habitat
Food	Enemies	"Is like . . . "

STEP TWO: DRAFTING

Discuss the differences between two animals; use the following sentence slotting pattern:

If I were a _____, I'd _____

and I'd _____,

but I wouldn't _____

because a _____ does that.

EXAMPLE:

If I were a dragonfly, I have 28,000 lens in my eyes and I'd fly backwards, but I wouldn't have a 12 inch wingspan because an Atlas Moth has that.

STEP THREE: REVISING

Add more details to each slot. Use stronger verbs and/or figurative language.

EXAMPLE:

If I were a dragonfly, I'd use the 28,000 lens in my convex eyes to see any movement on either side of me and I'd be able to dart forward, hover, or fly backwards like a tiny, iridescent helicopter, but I wouldn't sport a ruler-wide wingspan because an Atlas Moth does that.

STEP FOUR: EDITING

Check spelling and punctuation.

STEP FIVE: SHARING

Read your pattern aloud.

A RESEARCH PATTERN

USING DEBORAH GUARINO'S IS YOUR MAMA A LLAMA? *AND MARGERY FACKLAM'S* THE BIG BUG BOOK *TO CREATE A RESEARCH-REPORTING PATTERN*

Objectives: To focus on essential facts, display contrasts, and report findings in a question-and-answer format

Summary: In *Is Your Mama a Llama?* by Deborah Guarino, animals inquire about the nature of other animals' mothers.

STEP ONE: PREWRITING

Audience: Class members

Form: Contrast pattern/sentence slotting

Purpose: To show differences, use concrete details to support a main idea

Content: Animals/insects

Generate and Organize Ideas

Create databases for two animals. Use these headings; be sure to put at least 5 concrete details beneath each heading.

Attributes   Actions   Habitat

Food   Enemies   "Is like . . . "

STEP TWO: DRAFTING

To write about the differences between two animals, use the following sentence slotting pattern:

"Is your mama a _____?"

"No, she's got _____ and _____

and she _____."

"Oh, your mama is a _____!"

EXAMPLE:

"Is your mama a Monarch Butterfly?"

"No, she's got wings almost as wide as a ruler's length and a thick, furry body, and she vibrates her wings so she can warm up before she takes to the night skies in India."

"Oh, your mama is an Atlas Moth!"

STEP THREE: REVISING

Add more details to each slot. Use stronger verbs and/or figurative language; use phrases.

EXAMPLE:

"No, she's got wings almost twelve inches wide and a thick, furry body, and she vibrates her wings so she can warm up before she wings her way in the night skies of India."

STEP FOUR: EDITING

Check spelling and punctuation.

STEP FIVE: SHARING

Read your pattern aloud.

PROSE

A FICTIONAL LETTER

USING FRED GWYNNE'S PONDLARKER TO GENERATE A FICTIONAL LETTER

Purpose: To expand character awareness by using the letter genre

Summary: *Pondlarker* (Simon & Schuster 1990) is the story of a frog who thinks he is really a prince. He sets out to find a princess whose kiss can transform him; but when he finds her he decides that being a frog is not so bad after all.

BEFORE READING: READING TO WRITE

Consider these questions before reading *Pondlarker:*

Have you ever tried to be someone you weren't?

Have you ever imitated another person?

What is one thing that you really yearn for?

Read *Pondlarker* and compare your answers to the story.

STEP ONE: PREWRITING

Topic: A character from *Pondlarker* and his/her needs, desire, or fears

Audience: A character from *Pondlarker* or another person/character not in the story

Form: A letter

Purposes: To persuade, to inform, to complain, to request, to urge, to thank, to warn, to compare, to describe, to inquire, etc.

Generate and Organize Ideas

Make a list of purposes that letters can serve. Use the infinitive form: to _____

EXAMPLES:

to persuade, to inform, to complain, to request, to urge, to thank, to warn, to compare, to describe, to inquire, to R.S.V.P., to congratulate, to threaten, to apologize, to apply for a job, to recommend, to persuade . . .

STEP TWO: DRAFTING

Draft a letter from a character in *Pondlarker* to another character or another person (either in the story or outside of the story).

Definition: Letter

Letters are those things that we write—printed communications—and direct to a person or an organization. In a letter, the content and purpose(s) are always connected to the person (or organization) who will read it. In other words, the letter's audience, purpose(s), and content are tied together.

Guidelines for Writing a Fictional Letter

   a. Choose a character from *Pondlarker* and make a list of the different kinds of letters that he or she could write. Be sure to consider audience, content, and purpose. Also, be sure that the content of letter is based on the character's experiences and emotions (what he or she wanted, feared, was curious about, etc.).

   EXAMPLES:

   Pondlarker could write a "Dear Abby" letter to request advice.

   Pondlarker could write a "Dear Princess" letter to inform her as to why he chose not to receive her kiss.

Pondlarker could write a letter to another frog in a distant pond to warn him to stay away from princesses who have magical, transforming lips.

b. Be sure to give as much information as is needed to clearly convey the letter writer's purpose to the reader of the letter.

EXAMPLE:

(A letter asking for advice.)

Dear Bullfrog Mary:

      I think I am a prince who is trapped in a frog's body. I've heard stories about princesses who can kiss a frog and turn him into a handsome prince with beautiful, kind eyes. I would like to meet such a princess, but I have two problems. First, no one believes I am a prince even though I wear a cape, a plumed hat, a sword. They all laugh at me. My second problem is that I don't know where to find a princess who has magic lips. Should I stay in the pond and live the life of a frog, or should I begin a quest for a princess's transforming kiss?

      Yours truly, Pondlarker

STEP THREE: REVISING

- Is it possible to add more information (facts and examples) to your letter?
- Can you add stronger verbs, adverbs, and adjectives?
- Are your purposes clear?

EXAMPLE:

Dear Bullfrog Mary,

      I am a prince trapped in a frog's body, even though I wear a cape, a plumed hat, and carry a sword no one in my frog family and none of my frog friends believe I am a prince. They all laugh at me and call me names like "Prince Toad," "The Froge Who Would Be Prince," and "The Royal Amphibian."

      Now, I've heard stories about a princess who can kiss a frog and turn him into a handsome, kind-eyed prince. More than anything I would like to meet such a magic-lipped princess but my parents have warned me that to search for it would be dngerous. My question is Should I stay in the pond and live the flat life of a frog, or should I quest for a princess's transforming kiss?

      Please answer quickly, or I think I might croake.

      Yours truly,

      Worry Wart

STEP FOUR: EDITING

- Does the letter have complete sentences?
- Are all words spelled correctly?
- Are commas and semi-colons used correctly?
- Do all pronouns have clear antecedents?

EXAMPLE:

Dear Bullfrog Mary,

      I am a prince trapped in a frog's body. Even though I wear a cape, a plumed hat, and carry a sword, no one in my frog family and none of my frog friends believe I am a prince. They all laugh at me and call me names like "Prince Toad," "The Frog Who Would Be Prince," and "The Royal Amphibian."

Now, I've heard stories about a princess who can kiss a frog and turn him into a handsome, kind-eyed prince. More than anything, I would like to meet such a magic-lipped princess, but my parents have warned me that to search for her would be dangerous. My question is: Should I stay in the pond and live the flat life of a frog, or should I quest for a princess's transforming kiss?

Please answer quickly, or I think I might croak.

Yours truly,

Worry Wart

STEP FIVE: PUBLISHING/SHARING

Share your letter aloud and/or bind the letters together in a volume.

A SIMULATED JOURNAL ENTRY

USING CHRIS VAN ALLSBURG'S THE WRETCHED STONE *TO CREATE A SIMULATED JOURNAL ENTRY*

Objectives: To become aware of the nature and purposes of journals, use close observational skills, and engage the critical imagination by writing a simulated journal entry

Summary: *The Wretched Stone* (Houghton Mifflin 1991) is a series of journal entries by the captain of a sailing ship which record the strange experiences that ship and crew encounter after they arrive at an uncharted island and remove a "magical stone" from it.

BEFORE READING: WRITING TO READ

   a. What do you think the title means?

   b. What do you think the word *wretched* means? What might a wretched stone be?

   c. Choose one picture from *The Wretched Stone*. Do NOT read the accompanying journal entry in *The Wretched Stone*. (Cover it with a piece of paper.) DO NOT READ THE BOOK. (Wait to read the book until after you have completed the writing activity.)

STEP ONE: PREWRITING

Topic: Image content (from one of the pictures in *The Wretched Stone*)

Form: Simulated journal entry

Audience: Other class members

Purposes: To inform, express emotion, convey thoughts, question, and give information

Generate and Organize Ideas

Examine the image that you have chosen and generate ideas—brainstorm, web, cluster, freewrite, converse—that you could include in a simulated journal entry.

In other words, imagine that you are someone or something in the image and are recording your experiences, thoughts, feelings, ideas, reactions, etc. You may be anyone or anything you wish.

Be sure to give a day, date, and year. Identify who you are (age, gender, position). State where you are and why you are there. Be sure, however, to examine the details of the image; this should give you a rough context to place yourself in. Discuss anything else that seems important (problems, concerns, thoughts, events, etc.).

EXAMPLES:

(Based on the last picture in the book—two men dressed alike, each carrying a load of bananas)

Date: Monday, June 5, 1931

Identity: brothers, friends, coworkers at a banana plantation, sailors, zoo keepers, merchants . . .

Action: bringing food to family, a party, a ship, a store, a zoo; bringing a new discovery to town . . .

STEP TWO: DRAFTING

Write a simulated journal entry based on your observations of, and reflections about, the picture you have chosen.

Definition: Journals

Journals are notebooks in which people record the following kinds of things: personal experiences, daily activities, travels, observations, ideas, memories, sketches, insights, dreams, desires, snippets of conversations, interesting words and phrases.

Some well-known people who kept journals are Leonardo da Vinci, Jonathan Edwards, Meriwether Lewis, William Clark, Henry David Thoreau, F. Scott Fitzgerald, and Anne Frank.

For our purposes, we can use journals to record experiences, stimulate interest in a topic, explore thinking, personalize learning, develop interpretations, wonder, predict, hypothesize, spark the imagination, activate prior knowledge, ask questions, assume the role of another person, share experiences with other readers, and engage in purposeful research.

Types of journals include personal journals, dialogue journals, reading logs, learning logs, double-entry journals, and simulated journals.

Guidelines to Follow

Write a draft of your journal entry. Start with day, date, year. Be sure to focus on helping the reader understand exactly what is happening—or what happened—in the image you are using as a journal base. Be sure to include concrete details that help create a sense of time, place, person, and action.

EXAMPLE:

Monday, June 5, 1931

Today my brother Eugene and I made our fifth trip into the jungle just to bring back enough bananas to feed our pet gorilla. At first, the daily trips into the jungle were fun, but after a week, they are getting old. The banana bundles are heavy. But what worries me is that every day our pet gorilla keeps getting bigger and bigger. Today, the gorilla is over twelve feet tall—and has a hunger to match his size. I wonder if something in the bananas is making him grow?

STEP THREE: REVISING

- Check your draft: Does it contain clear, vivid, and concrete details?
- Does it contain enough information to help the reader understand what is happening in the image?
- Does it answer who? what? when? where? why?
- Have you surprised the reader in some way?
- Include a participial phrase or two in your entry.

Definition: Participial Phrase

Participial phrases are "-ing" phrases containing a participle and complements or modifiers. Participial phrases act as adjectives to modify a noun or a pronoun. Participial phrases usually tell what the noun or pronoun is doing.

EXAMPLES OF PARTICIPIAL PHRASES IN SENTENCES:

Coughing smoke, whining a horrid mechanical whine, and *creeping up the hill,* Sally's car looked like it was about to die. [The phrases in italics give more information about Sally's car.]

Waving quickly, smiling a toothy smile, and *batting her eyelashes as fast as the flaps of a hummingbird's wings,* Jane sauntered into the room. [The phrases in italics give more information about Jane.]

We finally found Reginald *sitting alone in his room, filling shoeboxes with pennies,* and *humming a tune from MTV.* [The phrases in italics give more information about Reginald.]

Max was a great cook, *mixing pancake batter at warp speed, juggling pots and pans like an expert,* and *churning out enough pancakes to feed a circus-tent full of people.* [The phrases in italics give more information about Max.]

EXAMPLE:

Monday, June 5, 1931 (participial phrases are italicized)

Aching from our repeated trips, grumbled to ourselves, and *to dread our task,* my brother Eugene and I venturedd again into the jungle ust to bring back enough bananas to feed our new pet gorilla. At first, the daily trips into the jungle were kinda fun (even though my mom made me and Eugene dress alike and all the people in our village laughed at us), but after a week, these trips are n't any fun any more. The banana bundles are heavy, and my shoulders are starting to ache. What's really rotten, though, is that every day our pet gorilla gcts bigger and bigger and demands more and more food. We run ourselves ragged just trying to appease his growing, gargantuan appetite. When we arrived home with our load today, we found that the gorilla, *eyeing the bananas* and *pounding the floor with his fists,* had passed the twelve foot mark—that's three feet taller than yesterday. I wonder if something in the bananas is making him grow? Hmmm. Maybe I should try one.

STEP FOUR: EDITING

Check for usage correctness:

- Are the sentences complete?
- Are commas and/or semi-colons used correctly?
- Does each sentence naturally lead to the next?
- Have you used parallel construction correctly?

EXAMPLE:

Monday, June 5, 1931

Aching from our repeated trips, grumbling to ourselves, and dreading our task, my brother Eugene and I ventured again into the jungle—our fifth trip today!—just to bring back enough bananas to feed our new pet gorilla. At first, the daily trips into the jungle were fun (even though my mom made me and Eugene dress alike and all the people in our village laughed at us), but after a week, these trips are getting old. The banana bundles are heavy, and my shoulders—and my attitude—are starting to ache. What's really rotten, though, is that every day our pet gorilla gets bigger and bigger and demands more and more food. We run ourselves ragged just trying to appease his growing, gargantuan appetite. When we arrived home with our load today, we found that the gorilla, *eyeing the bananas and pounding the floor with his fists,* had passed the twelve foot mark—that's three feet taller than yesterday! I wonder if something in the bananas is making him grow? Hmmm. Maybe I should try one . . .

STEP FIVE: SHARING/PUBLISHING

Read the entry aloud. Read *The Wretched Stone* to see how your entry compares with the corresponding one in the book.

A DESCRIPTIVE PARAGRAPH

USING JON AGEE'S THE INCREDIBLE PAINTING OF FELIX CLOUSSEAU TO CREATE A DESCRIPTIVE PARAGRAPH

Objectives: To describe a scene, support one general idea with specific sensory images, employ spatial awareness, use figurative language

Summary: Agee's book tells the story of a painter who wins a grand prize, is thrown in jail, and then is released

STEP ONE: PREWRITING

Topic: A dungeon

Form: A descriptive paragraph

Purpose: To describe

Audience: Peers

Generate and Organize Ideas

Here is a partial list of items that might be found in the dungeon into which the painter in Agee's book was held:

rusty iron bars

jagged stone walls

corners festooned with spiders' webs

stale air

the dank smell of mold

moth eaten blankets

flickering torches spewing smoke

flat straw bed

rats scurrying from cell to cell

tiny square windows

the sporadic laughter of the guards

Add 3 more:

_____

_____

_____

STEP TWO: DRAFTING

Use at least 5 of the details from the list in a descriptive paragraph about the dungeon.

Definition: Descriptive Paragraph

A descriptive paragraph is a unified group of (usually) 5 to 10 sentences that develops one central idea; the purpose of a descriptive paragraph is to describe—to create an image of—a particular topic. Like any paragraph, a descriptive paragraph should be unified, coherent, and adequately developed. Unified: Every sentence and every idea should relate to the main idea—the overall dominant impression—in the topic sentence. Coherent: The sentences and ideas should be arranged logically (usually spatially) and the relationships among them should be made clear by the use of effective transitions. A descriptive paragraph will accent sensory details and will often contain figurative language. Adequately developed: All of its facts and examples should prove the main idea in the topic sentence.

Guidelines

Start with a clear topic sentence: The dungeon was a _____ place. (Fill in the blank with one word that describes what you wish to emphasize about the dungeon; give one overall dominant impression: e.g., dirty, ugly, horrible, oppressive, Spartan, cluttered, frightening.)

In the rest of the paragraph, be sure to focus on specific details. Zero in on those things that you can see, hear, touch, taste, and smell. Use language that is concrete and specific.

SAMPLE PARAGRAPH:

The dungeon was a bad place. The light that came through the tiny window revealed bad stuff. Some people inside were singing. The floor was stained and the walls were made gray. Through the rusty iron bars of the door came the odor of smoke and the sporadic laughter of the guards. In one corner of the room was a flat straw bed full of bugs. The other three corners were festooned with cobwebs. The air was full of the smell of mold. This was a really ugly place!

STEP THREE: REVISING

a. Revise the paragraph by making sure all details support the idea in the topic sentence.

b. Check spatial arrangement: Does the paragraph describe the scene from left to right, top to bottom, inside to outside . . . ?

c. Be sure all details are strong and vivid and that they appeal to the senses: The floor was a great slab of stained, dingy granite.

d. Be sure the language is concrete and specific: e.g., The walls were composed of jagged, gray stone.

e. Use strong verbs, such as festooned.

f. Use similes, alliteration, metaphor, and/or onomatopoeia: In one corner of the room lay a flat straw bed which was infested with what seemed like all the bugs in the world (simile); shadow-shrouded guards (alliteration).

g. Use prepositional phrases to begin sentences: Through the rusty iron bars of the door issued the putrid odor of oily smoke and the sporadic laughter of the shadow-shrouded guards.

h. End with a concluding sentence that wraps up the paragraph: Clearly, this place must have been designed by someone with a nightmare-mind!

SAMPLE PARAGRAPH:

The dungeon was a horrible place a place not fit for humans. What little light managed to spill through the tiny square windw revealed details better left unseen the floor was a great slab of stained, dingy granite; and the walls were composed of jagged, gray stone. Through the rusty iron bars of the door issued the ptrid odor of oily smoke and the sporadic laughter of the shadow-shrouded guards. In one corner of the room lay a flat straw bed which was infested with what seemed like all the bugs in the world. The other three corners were festooned with cobwebs. The air in the place was dank full of the sickening smell of mold. Clearly, this place must have been designed by someone with a nightmare-mind!

STEP FOUR: EDITING

Edit the paragraph by checking to be sure that all sentences are complete, that there are no mechanical errors, and that all words are spelled correctly.

SAMPLE PARAGRAPH:

The dungeon was a horrible place, a place not fit for humans. What little light managed to spill through the tiny square window revealed details better left unseen. The floor was a great slab of stained, dingy granite and the walls were composed of jagged, gray stone. Through the rusty iron bars of the door issued the putrid odor of oily smoke and the sporadic laughter of the shadow-shrouded guards. In one corner of the room lay a flat straw bed which was infested with what seemed like all the bugs in the world. The other three corners were festooned with cobwebs. The air in the place was dank, full of the sickening smell of mold. Clearly, this place must have been designed by someone with a nightmare-mind!

STEP FIVE: SHARING

Read your paragraph aloud.

A PERSONAL NARRATIVE PARAGRAPH

USING JANE YOLEN'S OWL MOON
TO CREATE A PERSONAL NARRATIVE PARAGRAPH

Objectives: To reflect upon a particular personal experience, organize the experience into a written form, and learn the structure and elements of a personal narrative paragraph

Summary: *Owl Moon* by Jane Yolen (Putnam 1987) is a personal narrative in which a young girl describes a time when her father took her into the moon-drenched, winter woods to hear and see a magnificent owl.

STAGE ONE: PREWRITING

Topic: Personal experience

Form:　　Personal narrative paragraph

Audience:　Peers

Purpose:　To describe, reflect, recount, and inform

Generate and Organize Ideas

Create a lifemap of key experiences or answer one of the autobiographical questions.

Choose one experience that lasted somewhere between a few minutes and (at most) a few hours. In a journal entry, describe the experience.

STEP TWO: DRAFTING

Transform the journal entry into a personal narrative paragraph.

Definition: Personal Narrative Paragraph

A personal narrative paragraph is a unified group of (usually) 5 to 10 sentences that develops one central idea; the purpose of the paragraph is to describe an experience, give information about the experience, and recount the memory of the experience. Like any paragraph, a personal narrative paragraph should be unified, coherent, and adequately developed. Unified: Every sentence and every idea should relate to the main idea in the topic sentence. Coherent: The sentences and ideas should be arranged logically (usually sequentially) and the relationships among them should be made clear by the use of effective transitions. Adequately developed: All of its facts and examples should prove the main idea in the topic sentence.

Guidelines

Start with a clear topic sentence: One of the _____ experiences I ever had was the time I _____. (Fill in the first blank with one word that gives an overall sense of the experience; fill in the second with a phrase that conveys the overall sense of a particular incident.)

    a. Be sure the experience you are recounting is a brief one, one that took place in the space of minutes or (at most) hours. Avoid discussing experience that transpired over days, weeks, months, or years.

    b. In the rest of the paragraph, be sure to focus on details that pertain to the topic sentence.

    c. In the first part of the paragraph, set the scene, give background information, and introduce the people who were part of the experience.

    d. In the second half of the paragraph, describe the action, and show how the actions support the topic sentence.

[Topic sentence: One idea that controls the paragraph]

One of the scariest things I ever did was visit a house that everybody said was haunted.

[Discussion No. 1: Set the scene, give background information, introduce people]

It happened last summer. We wanted to see the inside of the house on the edge of our neighborhood. No one had lived in that house, and everybody in the neighborhood said the place was haunted.

[Discussion No. 2: Describe the action, show how the actions support the topic sentence]

We went to the house. When we got there, it was quiet. We were a little nervous. We went inside and saw that the house was a mess. We heard a noise. We ran outside. We never went back to that house.

STEP THREE: REVISING

a. Change the topic sentence: Fear is like a bolt of lightning: you never know when it's going to strike. And it struck me the day I decided to explore a house that was supposed to be filled with ghouls.

b. Add sensory images (concrete language) to the paragraph:
- to venture into the old, abandoned house on the edge of our neighborhood
- we noticed the dead silence that saturated the place under the baking sun
- When we crept through the door and took our first trembling peep, we saw a weed-infested floorless room, unplastered walls, a sooty fireplace, shattered windows, and cobwebs festooning every corner

c. Add thoughts and reactions to events and people:
- J. and I approached the house carefully
- we crept through the door and took our first trembling peep
- Our breaths caught in our throats

d. Use rich language: strong verbs, similes, metaphors:
- saturated the place (strong verb)
- breaths caught (strong verb)
- bolted out the door (strong verb)
- The loneliness and desolation of the place were like great grey clouds (simile)
- dead silence (metaphor)

[Topic sentence: One idea that controls the paragraph]

Fear is like a bolt of lightning: you never know when it's going to strike. And it struck me the day I decided to explore a house that was supposed to be filled with ghouls.

[Discussion No. 1: Set the scene, give background information, introduce people]

The "visit" happened last summer when my best friend, J., and I decided to venture into the old, abandoned house on the edge of our neighborhood. No one had lived in that house, which must have been fifty years old, for over two years, and everybody in the neighborhood said the place was haunted. The house itself was slowly falling apart. Most of it's windows were shattered; many of it's shingles had fallen off, leaving the roof with a leprous look. Paint, once a cool blue, was peeling off in great flakes exposing a dingy white undersurface.

[Discussion No. 2: Describe the action, show how the actions support the idea in the topic sentence: a scary experience]

That day, J. and I approached the house carefully. When we got there, we noticed the dead silence that saturated the place under the baking sun. The loneliness and desolation of the place were like great grey clouds and were so strong that we were afraid, for a moment, to go in. When we crept through the door and took our first trembling peep, we saw a weed-infested floorless room, unplastered walls, a sooty fireplace, shattered windows, and cobwebs festooning every corner. Just as we were about to ascend the stairs, we heard a low, moaning groan. Our breaths caught in our throats. Without a sound, we turned and bolted out the door. We never found out who or what made the noise because we never went back to that house.

STEP FOUR: EDITING

Check mechanics and usage. Eliminate errors.

STEP FIVE: SHARING

Read your paragraph aloud.

A PERSUASIVE PARAGRAPH

USING SHEL SILVERSTEIN'S WHO WANTS A CHEAP RHINOCEROS? TO GENERATE A PERSUASIVE PARAGRAPH

Purposes: To create a persuasive paragraph, support a claim with specific reasons ordered logically, match content and purpose to a specific audience, use a focusing sentence, and use transition words

Summary: *Who Wants a Cheap Rhinoceros?* (Macmillan 1983) offers a list of things that a rhinoceros could do around the house if it were a pet. For example, a rhinoceros would be a great "coat hanger."

STEP ONE: PREWRITING

Topic: Practical household uses for a rhinoceros

Audience: Mother or father

Form: A persuasive paragraph

Purpose: To persuade, to give information

Generate and Organize Ideas

Make a list of practical, household uses for a rhinoceros. Try to be as clear and as imaginative as you can. An idea can't be too divergent!

EXAMPLES:

A cheap rhinoceros would . . .
- be a great trash compactor
- be a good "guard dog"—a "watch rhino"
- be a moveable ring toss
- be a great neighborhood ride
- be an effective bodyguard
- be able to plough the garden

After you have generated your list, divide it into two categories: those uses that would appeal to mother and those that would appeal to father.

EXAMPLES:

Mother	**Father**
trash compactor	could hold up the car as you change the tire
move the furniture as you vacuum	could cut the grass
doughnut hole-maker	could plough the garden
could be a "watch rhino"	

STEP TWO: DRAFTING

Write a persuasive paragraph in which you try to persuade either mother or father to buy you a "cheap rhinoceros."

Definition: Persuasive Paragraph

A persuasive paragraph is a unified group of (5 to 10) sentences that present a limited topic and that attempt to persuade a specific person or a group of persons to accept an opinion (i.e., that frogs are the best animals in the world) or to perform a certain action (i.e., to vote for a certain candidate in an election). A persuasive paragraph (usually) begins with topic sentence, or claim. The topic sentence (claim) presents the main idea that the writer is trying to persuade his or her audience to believe or to do something; the supporting sentences offer specific, unified reasons that support the topic sentence.

When writing a persuasive paragraph, the author should always keep in mind these two things: persuasion can be based on reason and/or emotion; and persuasion is usually most effective when it appeals to the self-interests of the writer's audience. In other words, to write an effective persuasive paragraph, the writer should know what his or her audience wants, needs, or fears and then come up with ideas that appeal directly to those elements. In this way a writer can show his or her audience that they will benefit by believing the writer's opinion or by doing what the writer is asking.

Guidelines for Writing a Persuasive Paragraph

a. Begin with a topic sentence—a claim—that presents one idea that you wish to persuade your audience to believe or do. In this case, the topic sentence will be one that tries to get either mother or father to buy you a cheap rhinoceros.

b. Follow the topic sentence with supporting sentences; these sentences will offer reasons why either mother or father should buy a cheap rhinoceros. These reasons should appeal to mother's or father's self-interests; these reasons should also give facts, statistics, or examples that support the topic sentence.

c. Arrange the body sentences in an orderly way: Choose three reasons that would appeal to either mother or father. Arrange them from most persuasive to least persuasive, or from least persuasive to most persuasive. End the paragraph with a concluding sentence that is a call to action or that summarizes the paragraph.

EXAMPLE:

Position Statement: Claim
Mother, a cheap rhinoceros would be a wonderful addition to our house.

Reason No. 1:
A cheap rhinoceros would make a great trash compactor.

Reason No. 2:
A cheap rhinoceros would be able to guard our house when you are gone.

Reason No. 3:
A cheap rhinoceros could move the furniture for you while you are vacuuming!

Conclusion:
It is obvious, then, that the only logical thing to do would be to bring home a cheap rhinoceros—today!

STEP THREE: REVISING

a. Check your paragraph for the following:
- Is the topic sentence—claim—clear and specific?
- Is the topic sentence supported by at least 3 specific reasons?
- Are the supporting reasons unified, that is, do they all appeal to either mother's or father's self-interest?
- Is each reason supported with specific facts, statistics, or examples?
- Are the reasons arranged in order of importance—most important to least important or least important to most important?

b. Others ideas for revision:
- Include a focusing sentence after the topic sentence. This sentence narrows the focus of the paragraph and allows for a transition to the supporting sentences.
- Use transition words to connect each supporting idea: first, second, third.
- Make sure you have used strong verbs.
- Make sure your ideas are vivid and imaginative (not clichés)—they should be logical yet surprising.
- Feel free to change the ideas you came up with by doing more prewriting here.

EXAMPLE:

Mother, cheap rhinoceros would be a wonderful addition to our house [topic sentence]. Just considering the practicall stuff it could do [focusing sentence]. First, it could use its big feet to be smashing our soda cans all the time and helping us recycle them more efficiently when we take them to the recycle center on Saturday morning after I am done finishing watching my favorite cartoons. Second, it could keep our house safe by guarding it when we are gone because sometimes people might want to break into your house if they don't see no guard dog or nothing there. Third, it could save us time by both ploughing and fertilizing the garden. I really don't like doing them jobs I would rather be playing with my friends or doing something more fun. Because a cheap rhinoceros could the jobs better than anybody I think we should get one today [concluding sentence].

STEP FOUR: EDITING

Edit your paragraph by checking the following:

a. Are all sentences properly constructed? (No run-ons, no fragments—unless there's a reason.)

b. Are all words spelled correctly?

c. Are all verbs in the same tense?

d. Does each idea lead naturally to the next?

EXAMPLE:

Mother, a cheap rhinoceros would be a wonderful addition to our house [topic sentence]. Just consider these three practical things that it could do [focusing sentence]. First, it could smash our soda cans and carry them to the recycling center, which is something I know you don't like to do. Second, it could move the furniture around when you are vacuuming; that you way you won't strain your back. Finally, it could guard the house when we are gone, which is something I know you sometimes worry about. Because a cheap rhinoceros could do so many practical things around the house, I think that the only logical thing to do would be to get one today! [concluding sentence]

STEP FIVE: SHARING/PUBLISHING

Read your paragraph aloud.

Read Shel Silverstein's *Who Wants a Cheap Rhinoceros?* and compare your ideas to his.

A CONTRAST PARAGRAPH

USING MARGERY FACKLAM'S THE BIG BUG BOOK *TO CREATE A CONTRAST PARAGRAPH*

Objectives: To read and think critically, see and discuss differences, and create a clearly structured paragraph

Summary: *The Big Bug Book* (Little Brown 1998) by Margery Facklam presents information on a variety of large bugs.

STEP ONE: PREWRITING

Audience: Class members

Form: Contrast paragraph

Purpose: To show differences and use concrete details to support a main idea

Content: Animals/insects

Generate and Organize Ideas

Create databases for two animals. Use these headings; be sure to put at least 5 concrete details beneath each heading.

Attributes	Ections	Habitat
Food	Enemies	"Is like . . ."

STEP TWO: DRAFTING

   a. Create a contrast paragraph in which you discuss the differences between two animals. A contrast paragraph shows categorical differences supported by specific examples. A contrast paragraph contains a clear topic sentence that states the categories to be contrasted. Facts, examples, and concrete details then point out the differences between the two items in the topic sentence. Discussion/explanation sentences support the categorical assertions and details. Either the block method or the point-by-point method is used to structure the body of the paragraph. And the paragraph ends with a concluding sentence.

   EXAMPLE: BLOCK METHOD

   The Great Owlet Moth and the Walking Stick are markedly different in their attributes and abilities. The Great Owlet Moth is one of the largest insects, having twelve inch wings and sometimes being mistaken for a bird. The Great Owlet Moth also has the ability to detect the radar of its enemies, bats. In contrast, the Walking Stick has no wings, but does have a long skinny body. It cannot fly, but must walk awkwardly from place to place. It does not have the ability to detect radar sounds and must instead try to blend into a tree branch when it spots its enemies.

b. Choose 2 to 3 categories to contrast. Choose 1 to 2 details from each category.

c. Create a contrast paragraph; use first person point of view and divergent thinking. Begin with a topic sentence that asserts a preference for being one animal. Contrast at least two different categories that pertain to both animals—be sure to support the topic sentence. Give details for each category; follow each detail with a discussion that supports the assertion in the topic sentence.

EXAMPLE: POINT-BY-POINT METHOD

(Contrasting the Great Owlet Moth and the Walking Stick)

I'd rather be a Great Owlet Moth than a Walking Stick. Although the Walking Stick is the longest of all insects, the Great Owlet Moth is one of the biggest. I think it would be much more fun to spread my twelve inch wings and fly through a South American rain forest at dusk rather than have to strain to move my ten inch, skinny body in a wobbly motion as I walked up a tree limb in Australia. Also, while the Great Owlet Moth and the Walking Stick can both hide themselves by blending into the trees upon which they are perched, a Great Owlet Moth can do something that the Walking Stick cannot. If I were a Walking Stick and was spotted by a hungry lizard, all I could do would be to hope to blend into the matching bark. But if I were a Great Owlet Moth I could blend into the background and I could detect the high-pitched "radar" sounds of bats and dart away to safety before they detected me. So I'd rather be Great Owlet Moth rather than a walking stick.

STEP THREE: REVISING

a. Add more concrete details in the form of participial phrases, infinitive phrases, absolute phrases, appositive phrases, and prepositional phrases.

b. Change simple sentences into complex sentences with adjectival clauses, adverbial clauses, or noun clauses.

c. Use stronger verbs. Use transitional words such as although, but, by contrast, however, on the other hand, unlike, whereas, while.

d. Create a stronger voice—use personal observations. Be sure the topic sentence states the categories to be contrasted. Also be sure to discuss all facts and relate them to the topic idea.

STEP FOUR: EDITING

a. Check spelling and punctuation. Make sure all sentences are complete sentences.

b. Make sure all ideas connect.

EXAMPLE:

Even though both bugs are pretty cool, I'd rather be a Great Owlet Moth than a Walking Stick for two reasons: attributes and ability. Although the Walking Stick is the longest of all insects, the Great Owlet Moth is one of the biggest. Consequently, I think it would be much more fun to spread my twelve-inch wings and gracefully wing my way through a South American rain forest at dusk—sometimes even being mistaken for a small, grey-brown owl!—rather than have to strain to move my ten-inch, skinny body in a wobbly, choppy, rocking motion as I walked up a tree limb in Australia (I think the other bugs would laugh at me and call me names like "wobble-walker" or "brittle-branch-body"). Even more important than attributes, however, is ability. While the Great Owlet Moth and the Walking Stick can both hide themselves by blending into the trees upon which they are perched, a Great Owlet Moth has a secret weapon that the Walking Stick does not. For instance, if I were a Walking Stick and was spotted by a hungry lizard, all I could do would be to "make like a stick," hug a tree branch, and hope to blend into the matching bark. On the other hand, if I were a Great Owlet Moth, I could use my camouflage to blend into the background and I could use my tiny, secret ears to actually detect the high-pitched "radar" sounds of bats—my enemies!—and dart away to safety before they detected me. So you can see, there are at least two distinct advantages to being a Great Owlet Moth rather than a Walking Stick.

STEP FIVE: SHARING

Read your paragraph aloud.

POETRY

A POEM ABOUT DREAM-TIME

USING CHRIS VAN ALLSBURG'S THE SWEETEST FIG *TO CREATE A DREAM POEM*

Objectives: To access an alternative way of thinking and imagining, recount a dream sequentially, describe the dream world, understand the importance of setting, and use simple language to convey a complex idea

Summary: *The Sweetest Fig* (Houghton Mifflin 1993) tells the story of a dentist who receives magical figs as payment for his dental services. The magic figs make his dreams come true—but not in the way he expected.

STEP ONE: PREWRITING

Topic: Dream

Purpose: To describe sequentially

Form: Free verse poem

Audience: Peers

Generate and Organize Ideas

    a. List recent dreams you've had.

    b. Choose one (or create one—you may make things up!).

    c. Write it down in journal form (prose).

       EXAMPLE:

       I dreamed that I was standing on a tall ladder next to a tree that seemed to be growing in the sky itself. I stepped from the ladder to the tree with one foot. I grabbed a tree branch with one hand. I leaned back towards the ladder, still holding onto the tree with one hand. While this move was a little scary, I felt confident that I wouldn't fall, that the tree would hold me. I then jumped from the ladder to the tree, looked down, saw only sky below me. Looking down and seeing only sky was exhilarating, exciting. Then, feeling happy, I began to climb the tree. I don't know what happened to the ladder.

STEP TWO: DRAFTING

Definition: Dream Poem

A dream poem is a free verse (no rhyme or meter) that describes a dream. The dream poem, in this case, has two stanzas. The first stanza, like a camera zooming in, details the time and place(s) of the dream. The second stanza describes where the dreamer is, why he or she is there, and his or her reaction to events. The dream poem may end with a surprise—time, image, or place shift.

Guidelines for Creating the Dream Poem

The poem should be 2 stanzas long and should be a transformation of prose into poetry, one that trims and organizes. The first stanza should give the setting of the dream, where and when it takes place, and give clear, concrete, brief descriptions of the particulars of the setting.

   a. Each line should describe only one item.

   b. The first line should refer to a dream frame: dream journal, dream theatre, dream notebook, etc.

   c. The second line should give the time and place of the dream; the place should be general.

   d. The following lines should give more specific information about time and places in the dream. Use sentence fragments in lines 3 through 7.

      EXAMPLE:

      In a recent dream
      It's past noon.
      In the sky.
      Sometime before late afternoon.
      A great oak tree is suspended in the sky.
      The roots are thick and sturdy.
      The earth is far, far below.

   e. The second stanza should introduce you (the dream-speaker), tell where you are and—sequentially—what you are doing, and state (or suggest) what you are feeling. The last lines of the dream might surprise with a shift in time, place, image, or action.

      I'm on a ladder so tall I can't see its feet.
      I'm where I never expected to be.
      Alone, curious.
      I step from ladder to tree branch in a death-defying move,
      One hand holds on.
      I step to tree,
      Let go the ladder.
      I'm happy, I ascend.

STEP THREE: REVISING

   a. Strive to be accurate; you are describing the dream world (usually an unusual place), so your language must present it as an actual place. The place may be unreal, but the language must make it real. To that end, the language must be specific, direct, and concrete. Avoid similes and metaphor.

b. Try to condense. When restating the prose-dream-statement, work to eliminate words, turn longer passages into shorter phrases. Notice how the prose is packed into poetry:

I then jumped from the ladder to the tree, looked down, saw only sky below me. Looking down and seeing only sky was exhilarating, exciting. Then, feeling happy, I began to climb the tree. I don't know what happened to the ladder.

I leap to tree,
Let go the ladder.
Maybe it falls.
I don't know.
In a blue ascent, I climb into the secret of sky . . .

c. Use concrete language (nouns, verbs, adjectives):

It's perpetually bright-past-noon.
In a cerulean world.
An oak tree grows in the unoccupied sky.

d. Use techniques such as Alliteration (dangle down) and New Word Combinations (bright-past-noon, deft-step)

EXAMPLE:

In a recent scene from my dream theatre
It's perpetually bright-past-noon
In a cerulean world.
An oak tree grows, suspended, in the unoccupied sky.
The eminence of bark.
Wispy clouds scatter above.
The earth has dropped out of sight.

I'm on a ladder so tall I can't see its feet.
I'm where I never expected to be.
Alone, feeling acrobatic, curious.
I deft-step from ladder to tree, grab a branch,
Dip back—a death-defying move.
One hand only holds me from a pitch into oblivion!
I leap to the tree,
Let go the ladder.
Maybe it falls. I don't know.
In blue,
I climb into the sky . . .

STEP FOUR: EDITING

Check spelling, punctuation, mechanics, usage.

STEP FIVE: SHARING

Share the poem.

A MEMORY POEM

USING QUINT BUCHHOLZ'S THE COLLECTOR OF MOMENTS *TO GENERATE A MEMORY POEM*

Objectives: To compress prose into poetry, use descriptive and figurative language to convey strong memories, create sensory images that suggest an emotional reaction, and imply ideas and emotions without stating them directly

Summary: *The Collector of Moments* (Farrar, Straus, & Giroux 1999) tells the story of a boy who meets an unusual artist. The boy spends time with him, but after the artist leaves, the boy discovers that his paintings present exciting and unusual images. The paintings become, in a sense, the imaginative memories of the artist.

STEP ONE: PREWRITING

Topic: Personal memories

Form: A pattern poem

Purpose: To describe and recount

Audience: Peers

Generate and Organize Ideas

Create a life map of important experiences. From your life map, choose 10 specific memories, ones that are vivid and charged with energy and emotion.

EXAMPLES:

Great-grandmother making breakfast; exploring the woods behind her house; skulking in the secret passage beneath the stairwell

STEP TWO: DRAFTING

Definition: Pattern Poem

A pattern poem is a free verse poem that has a repetitive structure; as such it contains no rhyme or meter. In the case of this patterned memory poem, each stanza begins with with the words "I remember" and is followed by the presentation of a brief memory. The memory is conveyed in concrete and figurative language and presents an emotionally charged situation; the emotion is stated—it is shown.

Guidelines for Creating the Memory Poem

Choose 4 to 5 strong memories from your list in the prewriting section. Using them as a foundation, write a 4 to 5 stanza poem in which the first line of each stanza begins with the words "I remember" and is followed by the description of a brief, specific, concrete memory.

- Each memory should be a linguistic snapshot; it should be a memory of an event that took place in the space of seconds or minutes, not hours or days.
- Each memory must be described with concrete and figurative language. Abstract and general words must be avoided. The accent needs to be on particulars, not generalities.
- Each stanza must tell the reader exactly where you (the author) are, what you are doing, why you are there, and what your reaction to the event is.

- The emotional undertone of each memory must ring through, but must never be directly stated. Rather, the emotion/reaction must be implied and revealed though concrete details or figurative language.
- Each stanza should contain simple, straightforward language.

EXAMPLES:

I remember exploring the woods behind my great grandmother's house and finding a flock of quail.

I remember I didn't like math in school.

I remember cutting down trees for Christmas.

I remember the time I saw a man put false teeth in a glass of water to clean them.

STEP THREE: REVISING

a. Be sure your memory-images convey a specific scene and an emotional undertone. In other words, describe the situation with precise and vivid words (especially verbs and adjectives), and then offer your reaction. Do not state the feeling (e.g., "I was surprised"), but describe the physical sensation you experienced or describe the feeling you had by using a simile or metaphor.

b. Remember: Each memory is a snapshot and should be the description of an event that took place in the space of seconds or minutes, not hours or days.

c. Use strong, concrete language such as crisp yellow woods, their sudden up-rushing halted my heart, crunching snow, dragging home a tree, drop false teeth into a glass of bubbling water.

d. Use vivid verbs such as scaring up, halted, trudging, dragging.

e. Use similes (compare one thing to another with the words like or as): e.g., The lessons made my brain feel like a whirring broken fan.

f. Use alliteration such as halted my heart, left me longing, for fear my teeth would fly . . .

g. Use metaphor, such as for fear my teeth would fly . . .

h. Break the lines to accentuate words, images, and ideas.

EXAMPLE:

I remember exploring the crisp yellow woods
behind great grandmother's house
and scaring up a flock of quail.
Their sudden up-rushing
halted my heart,
took my breath—
left me longing for wings.

I remember mad math in 3rd grade:
the lessons made my
brain feel like a whirring broken fan.

I remember trudging through crunching snow,
dragging home a tree
I sawed-down for Christmas.

I remember the first time
I saw a man drop false teeth
into a glass of bubbling water.
I didn't open my mouth for fear
my teeth would fly,
and didn't drink anything that day.

STEP FOUR: EDITING

Check usage, spelling, and punctuation.

- Is each line grammatically correct?
- Are there complete sentences (or are there good reasons why some sentences aren't complete)?
- Subject-predicate agreement?
- Are all verbs the same tense?
- Do all pronouns have antecedents?
- Are commas used in the right places?
- Are apostrophes used where needed?
- Are words spelled correctly?

EXAMPLE:

I remember exploring the crisp yellow woods
behind great-grandmother's house
and scaring up a flock of quail.
Their sudden up-rushing
halted my heart,
took my breath—
left me
longing for wings.

I remember maddening math in 3rd grade:
the lessons made my
brain feel like
a broken fan.

I remember trudging
through crunching snow,
dragging home a tree
I had sawed-down
for Christmas.

I remember the first time
I saw a man drop false teeth
into a glass of bubbling water.
I didn't open my mouth
for fear
my teeth would fly,
and didn't drink
anything that day.

STEP FIVE: SHARING/PUBLISHING

Read your poem aloud.

A POEM ABOUT PATTERNS

USING GERARD MANLEY HOPKINS'S "PIED BEAUTY" TO GENERATE A PATTERN POEM

Purposes:　To use associative thinking to unify disparate objects, create images via the employment of concrete language, express wonder, use figurative language effectively, and make discoveries

Summary:　"Pied Beauty" describes many things in the world that are "pied" or spotted. The poem celebrates these spotted things because they reveal the workings of a divine artist.

PIED BEAUTY by Gerard Manley Hopkins

Glory be to God for dappled things—
*　　For skies of couple-colour as a brinded cow;*
*　　　　For rose-moles all in stipple upon trout that swim;*
Fresh-firecoal chestnut-falls; finches' wings;
*　　Landscape plotted and pieced—fold, fallow, and plough;*
*　　　　And all trades, their gear and tackle and trim.*
All things counter, original, spare, strange;
*　　Whatever is fickle, freckled (who knows how?)*
*　　　　With swift, slow; sweet, sour; adazzle, dim;*
He fathers-forth whose beauty is past change:
*　　　　　　　　　　　　　Praise him.*

STEP ONE: PREWRITING

Topic:　　Object of wonder

Form:　　Pattern poem

Audience:　Peers

Purposes:　To express wonder, to describe

Generate and Organize Ideas

　a. Make a list of patterns/shapes: circular, square, triangular, striped, dotted, etc.

　b. Choose one, such as striped.

　c. Think of many concrete objects that are examples of the pattern/shape you have chosen, such as sunrays, icicles, lines on a turtle's head.

STEP TWO: DRAFTING

Notice what Hopkins does in his poem:

- Form: A "curtal [shortened] sonnet," 3/4 of the original sonnet. The octet is six lines and the sestet is four and a half, compressed to ten and a half lines. Hopkins uses careful word choice to convey dense meaning in fewer words.

- Tone: Wonder, praise, awe
- Organizing pattern: "Dappled things," i.e., patchy in color, splotched, pied
- Special use of language using hyphenated words, similes, metaphors, and concrete language. Repetition of "le" sound in dappled, couple, stipple, tackle, fickle, and adazzle points to great variety in nature which stems from the Divine, whose beauty is myriad but unified and is past change. Divinity is expressed in and through nature.
- Underlying focus: The poem presents a sense of sensual delight with transcendental purpose—inscape, or the discovery of an underlying pattern that unites apparently diverse and disparate things.

Guidelines

Write a free verse poem (a poem containing no rhyme or meter) in which you celebrate items (in the first stanza) that are examples of one organizing principle, i.e., of one pattern or shape. Stanza 1 should contain a catalogue—list—of items that engender wonder in you.

- Be sure to use divergent examples; avoid clichés; use concrete language—no abstracts—and use similes and metaphors.
- Also use some hyphenated words; try putting words together that may not always go together.

In the second stanza, reveal what concept or principle joins the items in the first stanza. Begin with a few adjectives that connect the items in stanza 1.

I celebrate stripes:
sunrays coming down,
ice on a metal fence,
lines on the head of turtle,
fingers ready to play the piano,
words on a page,
headlights on dark road,
wings of birds.

These things may be strange, but they share something:
they are the lines
where my words of wonder sit.

STEP THREE: REVISING

a. Eliminate abstract nouns such as love, heaven, happiness, beauty, joy . . .

b. Use vivid verbs such as cutting, dangling, poised, pressed, slicing . . .

c. Put together strange, but imaginatively logical, verbs and nouns, such as ice-daggers dangling, headlights feeling forward, v's slicing south

d. Use similes and/or metaphors, such as slivers of sun slicing, ice-daggers

e. Use alliteration: Share the sudden sublime

f. Check linebreaks. Break the lines to draw attention to words, images, ideas.

STRIPED BEAUTY

I celebrate stripes of things:
slivers of sun slicing through cold clouds,
ice-arrows dangling from the crisscross of fences,

> *the head of a hand-sized turtle*
> *decaled with thin strips of yellow,*
> *splayed fingers spread poised*
> > *to pounce and play the toothy mouth of a piano,*
> > *steel tracks—rolled on, worn down, frozen in parallel—*
> > *shooting to vanish on the horizon,*
> *beams of headlights*
> > *on the brail of a dark dirt road,*
> *squawking geese wings of v's slipping south.*

> *These things, spare, superb, so rarely seen,*
> *are what my Imagination sees and says.*

SPOTTED BEAUTY

> *I celebrate spots and spotted things:*
> *dots on Dalmatians crossing the pocked street,*
> > *a polkadot dress on a snowy day,*
> *ladybugs, like freckles, punctuating the garden,*
> *the face of a golf ball,*
> *marbles scattered on the dappled rug,*
> > *freckles on my sister's cheeks,*
> *the sudden start of a cheetah.*

> *All these things, round, spotty, weird.*
> > *They're dots on the things of the world.*
> > > *Praise them.*

STEP FOUR: EDITING

Check mechanics: spelling, punctuation, usage.

STEP FIVE: SHARING

Share your poem out loud.

AN "I HEAR . . ." POEM

USING WALT WHITMAN'S "I HEAR AMERICA SINGING" TO COMPOSE A FREE VERSE, AUDIO POEM

Purposes: To use sensory images (especially sound), observe, use alliteration and onomatopoeia, understand the style of Walt Whitman's "I Hear America Singing," and read critically

Summary: "I Hear America Singing" offers a lyrical, free verse catalogue of singing-workers and their songs.

BEFORE WRITING: READING TO WRITE

Whitman's poem is entitled "I Hear America Singing." What "songs" or types of songs do you think he mentions? Read Whitman's poem.

I HEAR AMERICA SINGING by Walt Whitman

I hear America singing, the varied carols I hear,
Those of mechanics, each one singing his as it should be blithe and strong,
The carpenter singing his as he measures his plank or beam,
The mason singing his as he makes ready for work, or leaves off work,
The boatman singing what belong to him in his boat, the deck-hand singing on the steamboat deck,
The shoemaker singing as he sits on his bench, the hatter singing as he stands,
The woodcutter's song, the ploughboy's on his way in the morning, or at noon intermission or at
    sundown,
The delicious singing of the mother, or of the young wife at work, or of the girl sewing or washing,
Each singing what belongs to him or her and to none else,
The day what belongs to the day—at night the party of young fellows, robust, friendly,
Singing with open mouths their strong melodious songs.

After reading the poem, make a list of everything you noticed in the poem. Be specific.

EXAMPLES:

The words "I hear" are in the poem.

Lots of different people are mentioned in the poem.

Different songs are mentioned.

People are doing different kinds of work.

The poem doesn't rhyme.

The poem is a long (run-on) sentence.

STEP ONE: REHEARSAL

Topic: Place and sounds

Audience: Other class members

Form: Free verse, lyrical, cataloguing poem

Purpose: To describe

Generate and Organize Ideas

   a. Make a list of places that are noisy.

   EXAMPLES:

   School, football stadium, factory, street corner, airport, school pep rally, cafeteria, party . . .

   b. Choose one place that has particular and varied noises made by various people. List the people
   and the noises they make.

   EXAMPLES:

   School, teachers lecturing, first graders chattering, principal squawking, bus driver yelling . . .

STEP TWO: DRAFTING

Whitman's poem is free verse; it contains no meter or rhyme and consists of long, free-wheeling sentences. Notice the catalogue in Whitman's poem—the long list of songs and singers of songs. The catalogue suggests the idea that everyone has a song to sing and that freedom and democracy are found in the song of work.

Notice also that Whitman uses free verse (a long, free-ranging sentence) to communicate his idea that "life is a chorus."

Guidelines to Follow for Writing an "I Hear . . ." Poem

Write a poem in which you incorporate the noises and people you listed in Step One by doing the following:

   a. Write in the style of Whitman. Each line should be a part of a catalogue of specific people and the sounds they make at a specific place.

   b. Begin with: "I hear the _____ _____ing, the various _____ I hear." The first blank should contain a noun that refers to a place, such as a church, school, mall, football stadium, or daycare center. The second line should contain a verb ending in -*ing* that gives an overall sense of the kind of noise you hear at the place in the first blank. The next blank should contain a noun that refers to the various noises in the second blank.

   c. Use free verse and create specific, concrete images in each line.

   d. Use alliteration and/or onomatopoeia.

Definitions: Alliteration and Onomatopoeia

Alliteration: The repetition of the same consonant sounds or of different vowel sounds at the beginning of words or in stressed syllables. Example: Peter Piper picked a peck of pickled peppers.

Onomatopoeia: The formation or use of words such as buzz, snap, pop, sizzle, bang, or murmur that imitate the sounds associated with the objects or actions they refer to.

   e. Use noun-participle combinations to begin each line (after the first line): e.g., teacher singing, principal squawking, children chattering [to review participles, see the Simulated Journal writing activity].

   f. Do not use strong meter or rhyme; avoid similes and metaphors.

   EXAMPLE:

   I hear the school singing, the various noises I hear.

   The bus driver yelling as he pulls up to the bus stop.

STEP THREE: REVISING

   ■ Be sure you have used noun-participle combinations.
   ■ Fire weak verbs; replace them with strong ones.
   ■ Find synonyms for your noise nouns and verbs.

EXAMPLE:

Instead of the bus driver yelling as he pulls up to the bus stop, change the verb to one that's more vivid and add some alliteration. For example: the bus driver grunting a groan as he pulls up to the bus stop.

STEP FOUR: EDITING

Check your poem's structure: be sure it follows the format outlined in the rehearsal stage; be sure words are spelled correctly.

Try to streamline your poem: Make the images sharp and clear; use striking, sharp words.

EXAMPLE:

I HEAR THE SCHOOL SINGING

I hear the school singing, the various noises I hear.
The bus driver grunting a groan as he pulls up to the bus stop,
First graders chattering as they scamper into the school house,
The teacher singing her "good mornings" to lines of upturned faces,
The principal squawking the intercom announcements of the day,
The girls in the back row whispering their secrets and sighing their sighs,
Feet slapping asphalt as they shift and slide in games of dodge-ball,
Cafeteria mouths munching in chorus and hollering, hooting, and howling,
And, finally, the bell's sweet buzzing that tells me it's time to go home!

STEP FIVE: SHARING/PUBLISHING

Read your poem aloud.

EVALUATION FORMS

Alliterative Sentence Slotting Activity

_____   In the first blank place is a letter.

_____   In the second blank is the name of the character (or object) that does not begin with the letter in the first blank.

_____   In the third blank is an explanation—words, a phrase, or a sentence. The explanation contains words that begin with the letter in the first blank and also contains "correct" information about the character.

_____   The sentence has no spelling, punctuation, or usage errors.

Interrogative Sentence Slotting Activity

_____   The sentence has two animals or two objects.

_____   The sentence has two action verbs.

_____   The sentence has combined the animals/objects and verbs into a question that begins with the words "would you rather" and follows this pattern (one that offers at least two choices):

Would you rather _____ a _____ or _____ a _____ ?

_____   The question is parallel—both groups of words on each side of the word "or" must be structured the same way.

_____   The question has a prepositional phrase in it.

_____   The question has no spelling, punctuation, or usage errors.

A Research Pattern-Poem

_____   The poem follows the pattern in the activity.

_____   Each section of the poem contains correct information from the database.

_____   The poem contains strong, concrete words.

_____   The poem has no spelling, punctuation, or usage errors.

A Contrast Pattern

_____   The pattern in the activity has been used.

_____   Two items are clearly contrasted.

_____   Each section of the pattern contains correct information from the database.

_____   The pattern contains strong, concrete words and figurative language.

_____   The pattern has no spelling, punctuation, or usage errors.

A Research Pattern

_____ The pattern in the activity has been used.

_____ Each section of the pattern contains correct information from the database.

_____ The pattern contains strong, concrete words and figurative language.

_____ The pattern has no spelling, punctuation, or usage errors.

Fictional Letter

_____ The content of letter is based on the character's experiences and emotions (what he or she wanted, feared, was curious about, etc.).

_____ Clear and concise information is conveyed to reveal a clear intention of the letter-writer's purposes to the person who will be reading it.

_____ The letter is clearly organized: Each sentence logically leads to the next.

_____ Transition words work effectively.

_____ Strong language has been used, including concrete nouns and verbs, and figurative language.

_____ Sentence variety is present.

_____ No mechanical errors.

Simulated Journal Entry

_____ The entry starts with day, date, year. Its focus is on helping the reader understand exactly what is happening—or what happened—in the image being used as a journal base. Concrete details that help create a sense of time, place, person, and action are included.

_____ The entry contains clear, vivid, and concrete details.

_____ The entry contains enough information to help the reader understand what is happening in the image.

_____ The entry answers who? what? when? where? why?

_____ The entry surprises the reader in some way.

_____ The entry has one or two participial phrases.

_____ The entry is clearly organized: Each sentence logically leads to the next.

_____ Transition words work effectively.

_____ Sentence variety is present.

_____ No mechanical errors.

Descriptive Paragraph

_____ A clear topic sentence gives one overall dominant impression.

_____ The paragraph focuses on specific details. All details should support the idea in the topic sentence.

_____ The paragraph describes the scene from left to right, top to bottom, inside to outside . . .

_____ The language is concrete and specific, using strong verbs, similes, alliteration, metaphor, and/or onomatopoeia.

_____ Transition words work effectively.

_____ Sentence variety is present.

_____ No mechanical errors.

_____ A concluding sentence wraps up the paragraph.

Personal Narrative Paragraph

_____ A clear topic sentence gives an overall sense of the experience.

_____ The experience recounted is a brief one, which took place in the space of minutes or (at most) hours.

_____ The first part of the paragraph sets the scene, gives background information, and introduces the people who were part of the experience.

_____ The second half of the paragraph describes the action and shows how the actions support the topic sentence.

_____ The paragraph focuses on details that support the topic sentence.

_____ The language is concrete and specific, using strong verbs, similes, alliteration, metaphor, and/or onomatopoeia.

_____ Transition words work effectively.

_____ Sentence variety is present.

_____ No mechanical errors.

_____ A concluding sentence wraps up the paragraph.

Persuasive Paragraph

_____ The paragraph has a topic sentence—a claim—that presents one idea to persuade the audience to believe or do. In this case, the topic sentence will be one that tries to get either mother or father to buy a cheap rhinoceros.

_____ Includes focusing sentence, which narrows the focus of the paragraph and allows for a transition to the supporting sentences.

_____ The topic sentence is followed by supporting sentences, which offer reasons why either mother or father should buy a cheap rhinoceros. These reasons should appeal to mother's or father's self-interests; these reasons should also give facts, statistics, or examples that support the topic sentence.

_____ The body sentences are arranged in an orderly way: three reasons that appeal to either mother or father.

_____ The ideas are vivid and imaginative (not clichés)—they should be logical yet surprising.

_____ The language is concrete and specific, using strong verbs, similes, alliteration, metaphor, and/or onomatopoeia.

_____ Transition words work effectively.

_____ Sentence variety is present.

_____ No mechanical errors.

_____ The paragraph ends with a concluding sentence that is a call to action or that summarizes the ideas presented.

Contrast Paragraph

_____ The paragraph has a clear topic sentence that asserts a preference for being one animal.

_____ The paragraph uses first person point of view.

_____ The paragraph contrasts at least two different categories that pertain to both animals. Details for each category are present; each detail has a discussion that supports the assertion in the topic sentence.

_____ The body sentences arc arranged in an orderly way.

_____ The ideas are vivid and imaginative (not clichés)—they should be logical yet surprising.

_____ The language is concrete and specific, using strong verbs, similes, alliteration, metaphor, and/or onomatopoeia.

_____ Transition words work effectively.

_____ Sentence variety is present.

_____ No mechanical errors.

A Poem about Dream-Time

_____ The poem should be 2 stanzas long. The first stanza gives the setting of the dream, where and when it takes place, and offers clear, concrete, brief descriptions of the particulars of the setting. Each line describes only one item.

_____ The first line refers to a dream frame: dream journal, dream theatre, dream notebook, etc.

_____ The second line gives the time and place of the dream; the place should be general. The following lines should give more specific information about time and places in the dream. Lines 3 through 7 are sentence fragments.

_____ The second stanza tells where the author is and why the author is there. This stanza also gives the author's reaction to where he or she is.

_____ The poem should end with a "surprise" line—an image that is a leap from the other images in the poem.

_____ Strong concrete language is present.

_____ No mechanical errors.

Memory Poem

_____ The poem has 4 to 5 stanzas in which the first line of each stanza begins with the words "I remember" and is followed by the description of a brief, specific, concrete memory.

_____ Each memory is a linguistic snapshot; it is a memory of an event that took place in the space of seconds or minutes, not hours or days.

_____ Each memory is described with concrete and figurative language.

_____ Each stanza tells the reader exactly where the author is, what the author is doing, why the author is there, and what the author's reaction to the event is.

_____ The emotional undertone of each memory rings through. The emotion/reaction is implied and revealed though concrete details or figurative language.

_____ Each stanza contains strong concrete and figurative language.

_____ No mechanical errors.

Poem about Patterns

_____ The poem (containing no rhyme or meter) celebrates items (in the first stanza) that are examples of one organizing principle, i.e., of one pattern or shape. Stanza 1 contains a catalogue—list—of items that engender wonder.

_____ Divergent examples are present; there are no clichés; there is concrete language—no abstracts—and similes and metaphors.

_____ Some hyphenated words are present. Words may not always go together.

_____ The second stanza reveals what concept or principle joins the items in the first stanza. A few adjectives that connect the items in stanza 1 are present.

_____ No mechanical errors.

"I Hear . . ." Poem

_____ The poem incorporates the noises and the people who make them.

_____ Each line is a part of a catalogue of specific people and the sounds they make at a specific place.

_____ The poem begins with: "I hear the _____ _____ing, the various _____ I hear."

_____ The first blank contains a noun that refers to a place, such as church, school, mall, football stadium, daycare center. . . . The second line contains a verb ending in -*ing* that gives an overall sense of the kind of noise heard at the place in the first blank. The next blank should contain a noun that refers to the various noises in the second blank.

_____ The poem contains free verse and specific, concrete images in each line. It also has alliteration and/or onomatopoeia.

_____ No mechanical errors.

WRITER'S TOOLS

The following items are things that most writers use to spice up and energize their writing. These are especially helpful when it comes to revision. Which of these can you add to your writing to spice it up?

Repetition: The Employment of Words or Phrases More Than Once to Achieve Emphasis in Ideas and/or Rhythm

> *Beware, beware*
> *of the bear out there,*
> *Of the bear out there.*
> *The bear out there*
> *Likes to prowl and growl*
> *And paw the hair of hikers there.*
> *So beware, beware*
> *Of the bear out there.*

Alliteration: The Repetition of a Beginning Consonant or Consonant Sound

Peter Piper picked a peck of pickled peppers.

Betty Botter bought a batch of bitter butter.

Red robins rise on wings in a ring.

Onomatopoeia: The Use of Words That "Sound Like" the Audio-Images to Which They Refer

Bees murmur and buzz

Fireworks sizzle, crackle, zip and pop

Simile: A Comparison of Two Objects (One Object Must Be Concrete) Using "Like" or "As"

Water sprinkled on a hot griddle scattered like startled geese.

A rainbow is like a large box of crayons—stretched out.

A sun setting is like a gold coin dropped in a big vending machine on the other side of the earth.

Thunder sounds like a whale doing belly-flops in the clouds.

Metaphor: An Analogy Identifying One Object with Another and Ascribing to the First Object One or More Qualities of the Second

Our front lawn is our house's wide green moustache.

A mountain is an ice cream cone turned upside down.

A dream that is never fulfilled is a seed that dies in the ground.

Personification: Endowing Animals, Objects, or Ideas with Human Qualities

When the sun goes home at day's end, it takes a shiny key from a ring of stars and unlocks the door of night.

From constantly spinning and blinking, the lighthouse grew dizzy.

The locked door envied the elevator.

When I turn it on, the light on my desk casts a wide smile while the candle I just blew out sends up a slow shiver of lonely smoke.

Hyperbole: An Exaggeration (Often Takes the Form of Simile or Metaphor)

He took a breath bigger than a circus tent.

It was so cold that the house turned blue.

He had an alligator mouth.

Participial Phrase: Begins with Either the Present or Past Participle and Is Used As an Adjective

Shaking her head, wiping her eyes, and choking back tears, Emily said good-bye.

Jumping up and down, waving his arms, and shouting at the top of his lungs, Sid watched the rescue plane disappear.

Prowling the forest, growling a low growl, and sniffing the air, the lion zeroed in on its prey.

The tree frog, intoxicated by the sight of its own reflection in a puddle of water, sat for hours.

Suffused with a glow of delight, the tree frog gazed at its reflection.

Absolute Phrase: A Combination of a Noun or Pronoun and a Participle That Adds Information

Eyes wide, hands clenched, nostrils flared, Terry was angry.

Arms crossed, mouth closed, head tilted, Jerry was deep in thought.

The night being dark, we lost our way.

The battery being dead, the car wouldn't start.

Appositive Phrase: Set Off by Commas, This Phrase Further Identifies Another Noun

Edgar, the sad clown, tossed his oversized shoes into the air.

Syliva, the reclusive poet, spent many hours per day writing in a stone house.

Jameson, the musician who knows how to play an invisible harmonica, is scheduled to arrive in town tomorrow.

Prepositional Phrase: Composed of a Preposition Plus an Object of the Preposition and Its Modifiers, This Phrase May Act Like an Adjective, Adverb, or Noun

Adjective:

The frog in the next pond croaked all night long.

The frog with bulging eyes is really an enchanted prince.

Adverb:

The frog hopped onto the magical lily pad.

The striped turtle hissed raffishly through his lipless mouth.

Noun:

Beneath the bridge is the spot where discontented frogs gather at night.

Gerund Phrase: Uses the *-ing* Form of the Verb; It Acts Like a Noun

Catching flies is the specialty of the leopard frog.

Larry's favorite thing is reading comic books on rainy days.

Infinitive Phrase: Combines an Infinitive and an Object, and May Be Used as a Noun, Adjective, or Adverb

Noun:

To write poems about South American Ghost Frogs is Oliver's intention.

Yesterday, Oliver announced that he wanted to visit the secret lair of Ghost Frogs.

Adjective:

To alleviate his fear, Stan imagines dogs mumbling on his roof when he hears thunder.

Shakespeare's Viola had a face to suit every occasion.

Adverb:

Stan bought Laurel a car to appease him.

Max went to his room to sulk.

**Adjective Clauses: Modify (Add Information to) a Noun or a Pronoun.
Adjective Clauses Usually Begin with Who, Whom, Whose, Which,
That, When, or Where (and Are Set Off by Commas)**

Bullfrogs, which most people now associate with beer commercials, are actually magical creatures that fly on Tuesday nights. (Bullfrogs)

Dr. Giles McCroak, who is the country's foremost specialist on frog behavior, claims he was once a Ghost Frog. (McCroak)

We dashed to the mist-shrouded pond, where the bullfrogs were rising on magical lily pads. (pond)

**Adverb Clauses: Tell Time, Cause or Reason, Purpose or Result, or Condition.
They Modify a Verb, Adverb, or an Adjective and Begin with Subordinating
Conjunctions: after, as, before, since, until, when, whenever, while**

Cause/reason: as, because, since, whereas

Purpose/result: that, in order that, so that

Condition: although, even though, unless, if, provided that, while

Before we could scurry out of the house, we had to feed our frog a fine dinner of flies.

Many frogs jump on ceiling fans because they like "going for a spin."

We had to get the frog down from the ceiling fan so that we could clean the blades.

Unless I let my frog ride on the ceiling fan for at least an hour a day, he gets sullen and cranky.

**Noun Clauses: Function as a Noun and May Be the Subject of a Verb, a Predicate
Nominative, a Direct Object, an Indirect Object, or the Object of a Preposition**

That bullfrogs love to fly is something that most do not know. (subject)

This is what bullfrogs have told me. (predicate nominative)

Horace Mann does not believe that bullfrogs can fly. (direct object)

I will give whichever frog flies the highest the "sky-fly" award. (indirect object)

Listen carefully to what bullfrogs might say. (object of preposition)

Independent Clauses: May Stand Alone As a Complete Sentence

Last Friday Dr. McCroak taught us how to jump like bullfrogs, but we have not mastered the technique yet. (two independent clauses joined with the conjunction "but")

Before it takes flight, a bullfrog settles onto a magical lily pad. (adverb clause and independent clause)

Rich Language: Transformations from Abstract to Concrete/General to Specific

Not the birds flew away, but the green-headed geese cut a V across the mauve sky.

Not the fish were pretty, but the trout were stippled with rose-moles.

Not I was lonely, but I felt like a Dead End sign on a street where nobody lives.

Not the room was dirty, but the room was besprinkled with an antique dust and the corners were festooned with cobwebs.

Not I felt out of place, but I was a single flower growing out of the side of an endless stone wall.

REVISION GUIDELINES

Ways to "Keep Your Promises"

> *Every piece of writing contains an implied "contract" between the writer and the reader. The writer promises to deliver some literary goods: when all is written, something must be accomplished, be it the telling of a complicated story, the evocation of a mood, or the presentation of a brief observation.*
>
> *If you write a mystery story, you promise the reader a crime, clues, and a reasonable solution. If you write a surrealistic poem, you promise dreamlike images. A conventional short story promises character development, conflict, and plot, while an "experimental" short story promises only some movement of narration.*
>
> —Alan Ziegler, The Writing Workshop

1. *Conceptual Development:*

   Does the writing contain ideas, concepts, scenes, characters, and/or images that are clearly developed with examples, illustrations, facts, details, and/or dialogue?
   Does the writing contain vague or nonspecific ideas that can be replaced with more precise and specific ones?

   Are there large or small gaps in and among the ideas?

   Does the piece of writing fulfill its implied promises to the reader?

   Check the beginning and end of the writing. Try the piece without either and see if it loses anything.

   Where does the writing need to be expanded?

2. *Organization:*

   Is the writing clearly organized?

Do the paragraphs, scenes, stanzas, sentences, and/or images fit together in a way that is clear, logical, or effective?

Do paragraphs, stanzas, sentences, or words need to be moved so that the piece of writing can say what it really wants to say?

Does the writing contain unwarranted shifts in point of view (or verb tense, or imagery, etc.)?

3. *Sentences/Phrasing:*

Are the sentences and phrases clear and effective?

Are they simple and direct?

Are they too complicated and convoluted without reason?

Are the sentences repetitive in structure?

4. *Wording:*

Which words need to be "fired"?

Can weak verbs be sent packing and replaced with other verbs that are bulging with life?

Can adjectives be eliminated?

Can figurative language (metaphor, simile, alliteration, hyperbole, personification, onomatopoeia, etc.) be used in place of a general description?

Can concrete words replace abstract ones? (Rather than "The alarm clock woke me," perhaps "The alarm kicked my snoring brain awake.")

Does the same word or phrase appear too often in the piece of writing, wearing out its welcome?

Has too much description been employed?

5. *Cohesion/Transitions:*

Do word-links exist between paragraphs, stanzas, and sentences?

Do pronouns have antecedents?

Has passive voice been eliminated (except where it is used deliberately)?

6. *Sentence Structure and Spelling:*

Does the piece of writing contain run-on sentences, sentence fragments, or convoluted sentences that need to be amended?

Check spelling and punctuation (in the final stage).

7. *Writer's Tools:*

Check the "Writer's Tools" pages; can you add any of them to the piece of writing?

CHAPTER SIX

READY TO READ ALOUD SCRIPTS
Poetry, Prose, and Drama

The play's the thing . . .
—William Shakespeare, *Hamlet*

Oral reading fluency is critical to proficient reading.
—Prisca Martens, "What Miscue Analysis Reveals about Word Recognition
and Repeated Reading: A View through the 'Miscue Window'"

*Without a full experience in orality a person cannot truly
embrace an animating and invigorating literacy.*
—Barry Sanders, *A Is for Ox: The Collapse of Literacy
and the Rise of Violence in an Electronic Age*

Celebrate sound. The voice is the instrument. . . . Variety is the spice of speech.
—Pamela J. Cooper and Rives Collins, *Look What Happened to Frog*

This chapter contains texts that are ready to be read aloud: poems, stories, and Reader's Theatre scripts. The texts here can either be read to children or children can choose to read them aloud: they can be read separately or they can be mixed into a Reader's Theatre presentation.

In the drama section, there are three interactive scripts. With "Snake Loses His Dinner" and "The Further Adventures of Tom Sawyer" some children should be assigned (or be allowed to choose) character parts to read, while the remaining children should be divided into small groups. And in "Snake Loses His Dinner," some children will read the parts of the narrators. Each group will be responsible for coming up with ideas that will be added to the scripts as they are read. Before reading the scripts aloud, it is a good idea to give the children who are reading character parts time to practice; while these children are practicing, the children in groups will have time to come up with ideas to add to the scripts as they are performing.

Remember: The key to effective oral reading is to use vocal variety skills in energetic and enjoyable ways.

POETRY

What Is Poetry?

Poetry is a rainbow
fish that slips
your grasp
but jumps
into the
cool still pool
of your bottomless brain.

Poetry is a deep-
buried diamond
that you must
                    dig
                        dig
                            dig up
                                with
                                    the shovel of
your pen.

Poetry
is a pair of
shoes
you slip into
so you can
                tread
                    path of words
                            up
            beyond
                the moon.

Two Chants

CHANT #1

Sing me a song.
Sing me a tune.
Sing some jazz
        that'll make popcorn pop.
Sing some blues
        that'll make the bedbugs hop.
Sing some rock.
Rock my song.
Sing some rock
        that'll rattle the block.
Sing with a voice
        strong as steam
Sing with a voice
        horrible and green.

Sing, sing, sing
  until you fall into dreams.

CHANT #2

Come home, I cried today.
Come home, it's getting gray.
Come home, the clouds look mean.
Come home, the sky's a'spark.
Come home, thunder's rumbling.
Come home, the trees lean low.
Come home, before the lights go out.
Come home, come home, come home,
  there's a storm a'stormin in!

Going Inside: Two Poems

GO INSIDE

Going inside my head is like
going to the movies where lights flash,
children scream, music soars.
Other times it's like
walking down an empty street:
leaves blow by, a dog barks
in somebody's back yard,
cars sit sullenly in driveways.

GO INSIDE

Go inside a cat
and you will see
bird-thoughts flickering past,
rows of paper bags
for jumping in,
tons of tuna on fancy plates,
miles of cool sky,
a storehouse of string,
broken rocking chairs,
and dogs
the size of mice.

Declarations and Truths

Declarations

. . . We hold these truths to be self-evident, that all men are created equal, that we are endowed by their Creator with certain unalienable Rights, that among these are Life, Liberty, and the Pursuit of Happiness. . . .

Truths

I hold these truths to be self-evident:
that you shouldn't laugh and eat mashed
*   potatoes at the same time,*
that it's a bad idea to open a can of shook-up soda
*   in the car—*
that you shouldn't try to catch a baseball
*   with your right eye—*
that when your dog jumps on the bed to
*   wake you in the morning, its breath will always stink—*
that if you're the last one to take
*   a shower, there won't be any hot water—*
that most people really won't really under-
*   stand you—*
that M & M's should be vegetables and
*   broccoli should be junk food—*
that homework will always follow you home—
and that hiccoughs hit you just when you've got to
*   say something important—*

I'm Sorry, But Not Really: Three Poems

SLIPPERY WHEN WET

Forgive me
for letting
your hand
slip
through mine

It's such
a shame
that you
flopped face-first
into that
puddle of mud

THIS IS JUST TO SAY

I loved
pushing pushing pushing
you on
the swing

I'm sorry
you flew

over
the fence

I CAME TO SAY

I felt real
bad
about stealing
that bright
red red rose

and the yellow
one too

But I was
just passing

and they
called to me
by name

Opening the Door

When I opened the refrigerator door
a giant tomato hit me like liquid fireworks.

When I opened the refrigerator door
a carrot laughed at my red hair and
took my money.

When I opened the refrigerator door
a glob of Jell-O howled like a dog.

When I opened the refrigerator door
a drumstick played a rap beat
against a milk carton.

When I opened the refrigerator door
a bowl of rice scattered like a flock of birds.

When I opened the refrigerator door
the soup erupted like a green geyser.

When I opened the refrigerator door
the head of lettuce yelled, "Shut the door,
I'm tryin' to sleep in here!"

The next time I want to open that refrigerator
door, I'm gonna send my little sister.

Two Dream Poems

DREAM # 1

In my dream, it's around noon
In a foresty world.
There are trees and flowers everywhere.

Colors forever, green, red, orange.
No wind.
Trees above.

I'm near one big oak tree.
I'm alone.
The tree reaches to grab me.
I kick at it. I run.
I fall into a flower the size of a wheelbarrow.
The flower begins to close.
I push against petals. I close my eyes.
And then
I'm standing up, holding a small flower
In my hand.

DREAM # 2

It's very bright, spots of sun fall like candy.
I'm in the most beautiful place I've ever been.
On a lush hillside.
Deep deep green.
In the distance, a castle.
Birds are chirping.

I walk towards the castle.
The drawbridge lowers.
I saunter across.
I climb stairs.
At the top, I step onto a rainbow.
I smile and turn pink.

Poems That Wonder "If . . ."

IF I COULD CHANGE THE WORLD

If I could change the world, I'd delete
     the dog that howls every midnight,
the gang of scorpions that secret themselves
into my house like little Mafia guys,
tires that go flat on bicycles just as you're going down
          a steep hill,
my cat's breath reeking of ocean-flavored
          cat food as it purrs me awake

If I could change the world, you wouldn't
          have world-weary socks that sag like
          elephant-wrinkles around your ankles,
gray gunks of gravel that lodge in your eyes
          each a.m.,
summers that are shorter than a sneeze,
rooms that have to be cleaned and beds
          that have to be made,

and those weird noises rumbling in my
        stomach after eating my aunt's killer
        meatloaf.

IF . . .

If I were rain . . .

I'd splatter on windows
        and tap-dance—pitter-patter—on streets.

I'd turn potholes into puddles
        and give croaking frogs a shower to sing in.

I'd jump out of clouds
        with a million of my friends
        and drop without a parachute
        onto someone trying to dodge me below.

I'd sit on the petal of a rose
        and wait for the sun
        to evaporate me home.

Letter Poem

DEAR CINDERELLA,

While we're out shopping,
be sure to clean every
crevice and corner of the fireplace
with a toothbrush,
make the beds
using only your feet,
wash each of the fourteen towels
in a cup of water,
sweep the floor
in the house, in the cellar, and in the barn
with your hair,
clean all the hens' beaks
with a cotton swab,
feed the mule
with a spoon,
juggle the oranges
while you scrape the sides of the oven,
and iron the sheets
with a shovel.
We'll be home by three.
Love,
Stepmother and Stepsisters

Bean Magic

The beans begin to
quiver,

undo their enchantment
and shiver,
yawn a plant-yawn,
stretch and shake,
break their shells
in choral shatters,
grow green in staccato spurts,
flare leaves like fluttering wings,
fume, seethe,
burn with rage,
and erupt
into rocket stalk rising
gushing rushing roaring
bean magic soaring!

Rapunzel's Lament

The prince is here.
and he's calling to me from below.
I'll get my things, unfurl my hair,
but wait—what's this—oh no—
that's not the prince I had in mind;
that's not my prince at all!
He's certainly not very handsome—
and his hair looks a shock of straw.
Is that his nose, or a boot stuck on his face?
His clothes look more like hand-me-downs
than expensive, royal garb.
And what kind of horse is that for a prince
to ride: a mule spray-painted white?

Oh, he's calling to me again
with a voice like a rusty hinge.

So I think I'll keep my tresses bound up
and say, "Go look for someone
else with flowing locks
because I'm having a weak hair day."

Troll Toll

Here come those billy goats.
Trespassing
without warning
on my bridge—again.

Stamping, stomping,
tramping, tromping,
worry, bother,
harry, pester!

Those goats, those goats—
make me so mad!
If they cross my bridge one more time,
I may just lose conTROLL!

Letters-Colors-Emotions

LETTER-COLOR-EMOTION POEM

A is red,
> *the happiness of watching cardinals flock to the feeder on a foggy day,*
> *the anger in my mom's eyes as she glares at my baseball*
> > *and the broken window,*
> *the satisfaction of blasting my trumpet during a jazz concert.*

L is gray,
> *the boredom of vegetable soup and water for lunch every day,*
> *the dolor of dust settling on the furniture of an abandoned house,*
> *the listlessness of fog drifting through the streets.*

M is blue,
> *the loneliness of a single pair of blue jeans pinned on a clothesline,*
> *the satisfaction of the perfect snowball,*
> *the anger of hurricane waves pounding the shore.*

S is yellow,
> *the fear of staring into the eyes of a doberman,*
> *the nervousness of my shaking fingers as I open my report card,*
> *the joy at the top of the rollercoaster.*

MORE LETTERS-COLORS-EMOTIONS

D is brown,
> *the confusion of coffee stains, early morning decals on the kitchen table,*
> *the uncertainty of a tumbleweed summersaulting by,*
> *the certainty of a spoonful of chocolate pudding that I'm aiming at you.*

E is purple,
> *the regret of letting you borrow my bike when it still had two wheels,*
> *the pride of a peacock flaring open its wings,*
> *the determination of a chihuahua snarling*
> > *at a great dane.*

W is green,
> *the envy of a brick watching a hummingbird,*
> *the sadness of moldy Easter candy in a broken basket,*
> *the gladness of grins in a face-painting contest.*

In Defense of Late Homework

A flea flew up my nose
on my way to school today.
So startled was I

that I dropped my books
and the binder holding my homework.
To rid myself of the wee nose-invader
I sneezed and sneezed
and sneezed
so hard
that I blew out the flea.

But my downward draft
blasted both books and binder
onto a trampoline in a nearby yard.
The books bounced once,
the binder twice,
and caught by a great gust
of wind, they sailed up
somewhere
past the moon
of Jupiter.

So, if you want my homework
today I think we'd better
contact N. A. S. A.!

An Extended Metaphor: How Many Ways Can You Imagine a Pencil?

PENCIL ME IN!

A pencil is . . .

a toothpick for my imagination:
with it I pry loose
words wedged
in the crevices of my mind.

a slender shovel
that I use
to dig up
the rich ore of thought.

a conductor's baton
that directs me to make wordy music
as I scribble and scrawl
across the page.
a secret voice
that tells me
what I didn't know I wanted to say.

the microphone
of my mind, amplifying my thoughts.

a turbo-charged stickshift:
with it I leave
wordy skid marks burning across the page.

a weather vane
pointing out the way
my thoughts are blowing.

a wooden rocket
blasting off into
inner space.

the seeing-eye-dog
of my mind:
it keeps me from
getting run over
by speeding thoughts
in the highway of my head.

a pepper-shaker that spices up my
bland thoughts
in the bowl of my brain.

a wooden bucking bronco
that gives me wild-word rides.

a flashlight that shines on words
hidden in the basement of my brain.

a thermometer: when I'm hot with word-fever,
the lead level drops,
disappears,
and drains onto the page.

a slim tornado
whirling with words.

a short-wave radio
connecting me
to voices in the foreign soil of my
imagination.

the eyelash of a giant
thought.

the periscope of a submarine:
when I look through it,
I can see thoughts
steaming across my mind's uncharted sea.

a smooth branch
for chirping words to perch on.
a stethoscope
that helps me hear
the heartbeats
of secret syllables.

a magician's wand:
with it I can pull rabbits out of hats
and hats out of rabbits.

the stem of a flower
whose petals
drop
into the leaves of books.

a revolving door
never opening into the same letter-place twice.

the perfect dance
partner
linking my hand and head and heart.

a telephone line
connecting me to
the longest distances possible.

a metronome rocking
to the rhythm of writing.

an interpreter
that translates my befuddled
notions into words.

a divining rod
that leads me to the fountainhead
of my imagination.

a contortionist
bending thought into
the shifting, pretzel-like
shapes of poems.

a magnifying glass:
with it I become Sherlock Holmes
investigating the unsolved mysteries
of my mind.

a plough
that makes
furrows in my mind's soil
where I plant alphabet seeds.

King Arthur's Excalibur:
with it I cut through the chaos
of word-wars clashing in my mind.

Questions

Mole where did you get your blind face?
Did you wake up one morning and forget to put your contact-eyes in?

Coral Snake where did you get your brilliant colors?
Did you slither through a rainbow?

Cardinal where did you get your red?
Did you sleep in roses one night and get stained when it rained?

Giraffe where did you get your long neck?
Did you sneeze so hard that you stretched it forever?

Cheetah where did you get your speed?
Did lightning strike your tail when you were running?

Porcupine where did you get your quills?
Was your mother really a thornbush?

Turtle where did you get your shell?
Did you join a turtle army and forget to take off your helmet?

Bullfrog where did you get your croak?
Did you swallow a bit of thunder when you opened your wide mouth during a storm?

Peacock where did you get your bright-eyed feathers?
Did distant stars roll out of the night and land on your plumage?

Ant where did you get your antennae?
Are you really a bug from Mars and use them to phone home?

Whale where did you get your spout?
Was your great great great grandfather an ocean volcano?

Spider where did you learn to spin a web?
Did you have to earn a knot-tying merit badge from the Spider Scouts?

Red-Winged Blackbird where did you get your stripes?
Did you earn them as a squadron leader in the Blackbird Airforce?

Hummingbird where did you get your speedy buzzing wings?
Did you take flying lessons from a bumblebee?

PROSE

A Kitchen Too Small

Dirty dishes, piled-up pans, no room to cook, no room to clean!

"Husband," said the wife, "this kitchen is too small! This cocina is muy pequeña. Make it bigger!"

"Bigger?" asked the husband, "make it mas grande? I do not have time to make the cocina bigger. I must plant the onions and chiles."

"Onions and chiles can wait," said the wife, "but my cocina cannot."

The husband looked at the cocina. He looked at the pots and pans piled up. He looked at his frowning wife. "Very well," he sighed, "I will make la cocina mas grande."

In the morning, when the wife walked into the kitchen, she was startled by nine noisy chickens perched on the shelves and flapping their wings.

"Husband!" she cried, "what are these gallinas escandalosas doing in my cocina?"

"There was no room in the chicken coop," the husband replied, "so I brought them here, aquí."

The wife frowned.

The husband smiled.

And the gallinas escandalosas squawked cluck, cluck, cluck!

The next morning the wife found four fat pigs parked in her pantry.

"Husband!" cried the wife, "why are these cerdos gordos parked in my pantry?"

"There was no room in the pig pen," said the husband, "so I brought them here, aquí."

The wife frowned.

The husband smiled.

The gallinas escandalosas squawked cluck, cluck, cluck!

And the cerdos gordos snorted oink, oink, oink!

On the third morning, the sun had not yet come up when the wife heard terrible noises, escándalos terribles, in the cocina. She opened the door and spied a spotted cow, a stubborn donkey, and eight wooly sheep, all clamoring for something to eat.

"Husband!" she cried, "what are the vaca pinta, the burro terco, and the ovejas lanudas doing in my cocina?"

"There was no room in the barn," said the husband, "so I brought them aquí."

The gallinas escandalosas squawked cluck, cluck, cluck!

The cerdos gordos snorted oink, oink, oink!

The ovejas lanudas sang baa, baa, baa!

The vaca pinta lowed moo, moo, moo!

And the burro terco brayed haw, haw, haw!

"Get them out! Get them out now!" cried the wife, "ahora ya!"

The husband sighed. Waving his arms, he shooed the gallinas escandalosas outside to the chicken coop.

He led the cerdos gordos from the pantry and parked them in the pig pen.

He herded the ovejas lanudas to the sheep pen.

He drove the vaca pinta and the burro terco to the barn.

When he returned, the cocina was peaceful and quiet, pacífica y tranquila.

The wife looked at her husband and exclaimed, "Look how big it is! It is muy grande!"

"Sí, sí," agreed the husband.

"Yes," said the wife, "this cocina is not too big. It is not too small. It is just right."

The husband smiled.

Then the wife frowned and said, "But the bedroom, la alcoba, is too small. It is muy pequeña. I want you to make it bigger. Make la alcoba mas grande."

Before her husband could speak, the wife added, "And this time, leave the animals outside."

From the barnyard, the gallinas escandalosas squawked cluck, cluck, cluck.

The cerdos gordos snorted oink, oink, oink.

The ovejas lanudas sang baa, baa, baa.

The vaca pinta lowed moo, moo, moo.

The burro terco brayed haw, haw, haw.

The husband frowned.

And the wife smiled.

GLOSSARY

Spanish	English
cocina	kitchen
muy	very
pequeña	small
mas	much
grande	bigger
aquí	here
nueve	nine
escandaloso	noisy
gallinas	chickens

quatro	four
cerdos	pigs
gordos	fat
ocho	eight
ovejas	sheep
lanudas	wooly
vaca	cow
pinta	spotted
burro	donkey
terco	stubborn
escándalos	noises
terribles	terrible
estos	these
animales	animals
ahora ya	now (emphatic)
es	is
sí	yes
y	and
pacîfica	peaceful
tranquila	quiet, tranquil
perfecta	perfect
alcoba	bedroom

The Day of the 'Dozer

Spring had come. Wispy clouds drifted across the sky. Trees sprouted green buds. New grass stretched towards the sun. Flowers bloomed like a rainbow carpet covering the ground.

Far above the ground, inside a hollow tree, Mama Wood Duck fussed over her nest of ducklings.

Standing on wobbly legs, the ducklings peeped and chirped. They nudged and budged, pushed and shoved, and hopped and bumped.

Mama Duck knew it was time to leave the nest. She flew out of the hole in the tree and landed on the ground. She called to her ducklings to follow her.

The ducklings crept to the edge of the hole and looked down.

Below, Mama Duck was only a tiny patch of color.

Mama Duck called to her ducklings again.

The ducklings did not move. They peeped, but they did not jump.

Mama Duck called one more time.

The oldest duckling climbed to the edge of the hole and looked down.

He opened his tiny wings and jumped out of the hole. He flapped his wings, but did not fly. Round and round he tumbled towards the forest floor. When he hit the ground, he bounced once and rolled safely to Mama Duck.

One by one, the other ducklings popped out of the hole. Like their brother, they hit the ground and bounced like fuzzy, feathery balls. After the ducklings stopped bouncing, they all gathered around Mama Duck.

Mama Duck counted her ducklings. She stretched her neck. She looked to the right and to the left. She even looked behind her.

One of her ducklings was missing!

Mama Duck looked up. Perched on the edge of the hole was her youngest duckling.

Mama Duck called to him.

The duckling did not move.

Mama Duck called a second time.

Still, her duckling did not move. A tiny shiver ruffled his feathers.

Mama Duck stamped her foot. She flapped her wings and squawked a long and loud squawk.

As the duckling opened his mouth to peep, a sudden roaring-buzzing-grinding noise erupted in the forest.

It was a noise the duckling had never heard before.

It was a noise that no forest animal made.

It was a harsh and powerful noise.

And it was not a friendly noise at all.

Then, the noise stopped.

Silence fell over the forest.

And nearby, a tall tree fell to the ground, landing with a great thud.

The roaring-buzzing-grinding started again.

This time it was closer!

It was louder and harsher.

And then, silence.

The duckling trembled.

A huge tree crashed to the ground closer to the duckling's tree.

Once more, the roaring-buzzing-grinding started. It grew closer and louder, and louder and closer.

The duckling peeped a tiny peep.

He gripped the edge of the hole more firmly.

He felt the whole tree shiver, quiver, and shake.

And the duckling jumped.

He tumbled over and over, flapping his wings.

He fell and fell and fell.

When he hit the ground, he bounced once, and bounced again.

He then scurried to Mama Duck.

Mama Duck and her ducklings scampered away from the tree. They plopped into the safety of the pond on the edge of the forest. The youngest duckling was the last to jump in.

The roaring-buzzing-grinding noise cut through the forest again.

Mama Duck and her ducklings turned to see tree after tree tip, pitch, and crash to the ground. The falling trees made sounds like great animals in pain.

The forest shook.

The ground vibrated.

Even the pond quivered.

Mama Duck and her ducklings watched giant yellow machines belching black smoke grind their way to the edge of the pond.

There they stopped.

Behind them the forest lay shattered and broken.

The machine shuddered to silence.

The door of the machine opened.

And down stepped a man.

The Last Breeze of Summer

I was lounging in my backyard treehouse late last September when I was roused by the stirrings of the wind. I looked up in time to catch sight of the last breeze of summer skipping low on the sky, heading east, slipping out of town with the last bloom of flowers.

Leaves had already begun to fall like lifeless hands. I heard the breeze sigh; it was a quiet mournful sigh. The sigh was so near me that I could feel it slip across my face. So surprised was I that I gasped a small gasp; and as I did I gulped the breeze into my lungs. I felt an immediate glow, like a piece of the sun had suddenly set in my chest.

Holding my breath, I swung down from the treehouse, scurried across the yard, dashed into my house, and scampered into my room where I coughed one great cough and released the last breeze of summer from my chest. The breeze leapt out of me, filled my room with a subdued and hazy warmth. As it slowly whirled around my room, I felt it sift though my hair and whoosh against my face.

For the next few days and nights the breeze stayed with me. It helped me keep my room clean by blowing the dust out the window. It spun my mobiles with glee and it tossed my cards around the room in an endless game of 52 pickup.

Because the weather outside had grown gray and cold, the breeze and I stayed in and played games. I made a small kite and the breeze took it and tossed it from one of its windy hands to the other. The breeze and I also played catch with balloons and cotton balls, and at night the breeze lulled me to sleep with airy stories of the origin of the wind and with dramas of dust storms.

When winter roared in on an icy breath, the breeze grew frightened. It swirled around the room like a trapped animal. I tried to calm it by bringing in pictures of the sun, but the breeze only wailed and howled, becoming a vortex of fear and anger. I even brought in a fan to keep the breeze company, but the breeze smashed the fan, tore it to bits, and then unleashed a tornadic fury against my room. It hurled my toys against the wall; it overturned my bed, and it upended my dresser. It finally grabbed me and spun me in berserk circles, making me so dizzy that I couldn't tell which way was up or down. I was like a puppet spun by a maniacal puppeteer.

When the breeze finally dropped me, I managed to crawl out of the room and slam the door behind me, trapping the breeze inside. I hurried to the garage, grabbed my dad's shop vac, his mighty industrial-strength vacuum cleaner.

Cautiously, I crept back to my room, with shop vac in tow, opened my door, switched on the mighty vacuum and caught the mad breeze with the nozzle. Before the breeze knew what hit it, I used the shop vac to suck it inside.

When next summer comes around, I'll open the shop vac and release the breeze to the warm winds. Until then, though, I think I might try to see how it would be to bring home a couple of snowflakes.

After all, snowflakes are soft and delicate, and I'm sure they wouldn't cause any trouble at all.

DRAMA

Snake Loses His Dinner:
An Interactive Reader's Theatre Script

Characters:	*Three Narrators, Snake, Mouse, Coyote, and ten small groups.*
Narrator 1:	It was a very hot day. In fact it was so hot that:
Group 1:	Tell four ways to describe a hot day.
Narrator 1:	It was so hot that snake crawled under a rock to find some shade. Snake fell asleep. The hot wind covered the rock with sand. Snake was trapped!
Narrator 2:	A mouse came along and heard snake calling for help.
Group 2:	Tell what snake will say—but do not tell mouse who you are.
Mouse:	Who is there?
Snake:	I am snake and I am trapped!

Mouse:	You are a snake. Why should I help you? Snakes eat mice.
Snake:	You should help me because:
Group 3:	Tell three reasons snake will give.
Mouse:	Very well. I will help you.
Narrator 2:	The mouse dug and dug. She set the snake free.
Mouse:	My, I didn't know how you looked. But I see that you are:
Group 4:	Tell four words to describe the snake.
Narrator 1:	The snake slithered towards the mouse. He looked very hungry.
Snake:	Thank you for letting me out little mouse. Now I am going to eat you!
Mouse:	No, no, please don't eat me. You must not eat me because:
Group 5:	Tell three reasons the mouse will give.
Narrator 1:	The snake slithered closer and closer. He was about to eat the mouse.
Narrator 3:	Just then, coyote came along. Mouse knew it was coyote because of coyote's:
Group 6:	Tell words to describe coyote.
Coyote:	What is going on here?
Mouse:	I set snake free. Now he is going to eat me.
Coyote:	You mean the snake set you free, little mouse?
Snake:	No, no, the mouse set me free.
Coyote:	I do not understand. You mean mouse was trapped under the rock? And snake set her free?
Snake:	No, I was trapped under the rock.
Coyote:	I still do not understand. I think that you should show me.
Snake:	Very well. I will.
Group 7:	Describe how snake crawls under the rock.
Coyote:	Now I understand. Snake was trapped under the rock. The mouse set you free.
Snake:	Yes, that is what I told you. Now, let me out.
Coyote:	I think I will let mouse decide if she should let you out. Good bye.
Narrator 3:	The coyote winked at the mouse and then hurried away.
Snake:	Mouse, if you let me out, I will not eat you. Instead, I will give you:
Group 8:	Tell five things snake says he will give to the mouse this time.
Mouse:	Well, I think that I will . . .
Group 9:	Tell what mouse says and does.
Narrator 2:	The mouse then went on her way.
Narrator 1:	And the snake . . .
Group 10:	Tell what happens to the snake (no violence).

The Travelers and the Bear: Prose Version

Two friends were traveling on the same road together when they met with a bear. The one, in great fear, without a thought of his companion, climbed up into a tree and hid himself. The other, seeing that he had no chance singlehanded against the bear, had nothing left but to throw himself on the ground and feign to be dead, for he had heard that a bear will never touch a dead body. As he thus lay, the bear came up to his head, muzzling and snuffing at his nose, and ears, and heart, but the man immovably held his breath and the beast, supposing him to be dead, walked away. When the bear was fairly out of sight, his companion came down out of the tree and asked what it was that the bear whispered to him, "For," he said, "I observed the bear put its mouth very close to your ear." "Why," replied the other, "it was no great secret; the bear only bade me have a care how I kept company with those who, when they get into a difficulty, leave their friends in the lurch."

The Travelers and the Bear: A Reader's Theatre Script

Characters:	*Three Narrators, Friend 1, Friend 2, Bear*
Narrator 1:	Two friends were traveling on the same road together when they met
Friends 1 & 2:	a bear.
Narrator 1:	The one
Friend 1:	in great fear
Narrator 1:	without thought of his companion
Friend 1:	climbed up into a tree
Narrator 1:	and hid himself.
Narrator 2:	The other, seeing he had
Friend 2:	no chance singlehanded against the bear
Narrator 2:	had nothing left but to throw himself
Friend 2:	on the ground and feign dead
Narrator 2:	for he had heard
Friend 2:	that a bear will never touch a dead body.
Narrator 2:	As he thus lay
Narrator 3:	the bear came up to his head
Bear:	muzzling and snuffing at his nose, and ears, and heart
Narrator 2:	but the man immovably held his breath
Narrator 3:	and the beast
Bear:	supposing him to be dead
Narrator 3:	walked away.
Friend 1:	When the bear was fairly out of sight
Narrator 1:	his companion came down out of the tree and asked
Friend 1:	what it was that the bear whispered to him. "For,"
Narrator 1:	he said
Friend 1:	"I observed the bear put its mouth very close to your ear."
Friend 2:	"Why"
Narrator 2:	replied the other
Friend 2:	"it was no great secret; the bear only bade me have a care how I kept company with those who, when they get into a difficulty, leave their friends in the lurch."

A Rain Story: A Group and Solo Script

Parts:	*Group A, Group B, and Solos 1–12.*
Group A:	I'll tell you a story about rain and glory
	And now my story's begun.
	I'll tell you another about
	Terrible weather
	And now my story is done.

Group B:	(begin when group A says "begun")
	I'll tell you a story about rain and glory
	And now my story's begun.
	I'll tell you another about
	Terrible weather
	And now my story is done.
Group A:	Back and forth. Back and forth.
	Back and forth. Back and forth.
Group A:	In the dark dark night
Group B:	Is the thick gray sky.
Group A:	In the thick gray sky
Group B:	Is a thick gray cloud.
Group A:	In the thick gray cloud
Group B:	Is a thick gray sound:
Groups A & B:	Thunder!
Group A:	Crash! (clap hands once)
Group B:	Crash, crash! (clap hands twice)
Groups A & B:	Kaboom! (clap hands three times)
Group B:	Softly now, softly now, softly now,
	And sing:
Groups A & B:	It's raining, it's pouring,
	The old man is snoring.
Group B:	Use the words,
	Say the words,
	Say them
	Again and again:
Solo 1:	Rainy, wet
Solo 2:	Misty, moist
Solo 3:	Soppy, drenched
Solo 4:	Drippy, damp
Group A:	The rain in Spain stays mainly on the plain.
Group B:	The sleet in St. Pete stays mainly on the street.
Groups A & B:	Rain, rain go away
	Come again another day.
	Let the sun come out to stay
	So we can dash and play.
Solo 5:	Rain makes the grass grow.
Solo 6:	Rain makes the flowers bloom.
Solo 7:	Rain makes it hard to hoe.
Solo 8:	Rain keeps me in my room.
Group A:	Raindrops keep falling
Group B:	Falling, falling, falling
Group A:	Behind every cloud is a silver lining.
Group B:	March winds bring April showers

	And April showers bring May flowers.
All:	And Mayflowers bring Pilgrims!
Solo 9:	My heart leaps up
Solo 10:	When I behold a rainbow in the sky!
Solo 11:	At the end of every rainbow is a pot of gold!
Group A:	And now my story is done.
Group B:	And now my story is done.
Solo 12:	Don't forget your umbrella!
All:	And now my story is done!

A Mouse and Sea Story / Un Cuento del Ratón y Mar

Parts:	*Group A, Group B, and All*
Group A:	I'll tell you a story about the mice and the sea,
	And now my story's begun.
Group B:	I'll tell you another about
	la arena y el sol,
	Now my cuento is begun.
Group A:	I'll tell you a story about
	el ratón y el mar,
	And now my cuento is begun.
Group B:	I'll tell you another about the sand and the sun.
	And now my story is begun.
Group A:	Back and forth.
	Back and forth.
Group B:	Back and forth.
	Back and forth.
Group A:	On the sandy shore
Group B:	Sheep sleep and snore
Group A:	And a slow ship sends smoke soaring into the sky!
Group B:	Humo in the sky!
	¡Mira, mira! The sea-serpent has a shoe on its tail!
Group A:	Un zapato on its tail?
Group B:	Sí! And the sightless, skinny skeleton plays a simple song
Group A:	On the shiny, sweet saxaphone.
Group B:	On the saxofón dulce y brillante!
All:	Softly now, softly now,
	softly now, and say:
Group A:	Sally sells seashells
	on the sandy seashore!
Group B:	Conchas on the sandy seashore.
All:	Use the words,
	use las palabras,
	Say them again and again:

Group A:	Snow on the summit.
Group B:	Nieve en la cima.
Group A:	Shells in the sand.
Group B:	Conchas en la arena.
Group A:	But the mice,
	the mice
	are twice as nice.
Group B:	And one mouse
	wears a mask!
All:	The Mice, the mice
	are here today—
	they're here
	to stay and play.
Group A:	The magnet,
	the missle,
	and the massive mushroom
Group B:	El imán, el misil, y
	el hongo gigante
Group A:	Mice-toys
	made for playing.
Group B:	The moose
	on the map.
Group A:	Alce en la mapa.
Group B:	The mermaid in the sea.
Group A:	La sirena en el mar.
Group B:	She's in the sea I see!
All:	Sî, she's in the sea!
Group A:	My heart leaps up
Group B:	When I see
	a monocle
	on a mouse.
Group A:	Un monocúlo en el ratón?
All:	Claro que sí! Of course!
Group B:	Mouse.
Group A:	Ratón.
Group B:	Mouse.
Group A:	Ratón.
Group B:	Mouse.
Group A:	Ratón, ratón!
All:	Behind every mouse
	is un ratón!
Group A:	"Whoosh" goes the waves!
Group B:	"Squeek" go the mice!

Group A:	"Hiss" goes the snake.
Group B:	"Baa" go the sheep.
Group A:	"Grrr" goes the monster.
All:	Does el ratón make a noise?
Group A:	And now my story is done.
Group B:	And now my cuento is done.
All:	And now, my story is done!

GLOSSARY

Spanish	*English*
Un	a
Cuento	story
Del	of
Ratónes	mice
Y	and
Mar	sea
La arena	sand
El sol	sun
Humo	smoke
¡Mira!	Look!
Un zapato	a shoe
Saxofón	saxaphone
Dulce	sweet
Brillante	shiny
Conchas	seashells
Las palabras	words
Nieve	snow
En	on
La cima	the summit
El imán	magnet
El misil	missle
El hongo	mushroom
Gigante	massive
Alce	moose
La mapa	map
La sirena	mermaid
Un monocúlo	monocle
Claro que sí!	Of course!

The Further Adventures of Tom Sawyer: An Interactive Reader's Theatre Script

Characters:	*Tom Sawyer, Aunt Polly, Cousin Sid, Huck Finn, Narrator, and 10 Audience–Author Groups.*
Narrator:	Tom and Aunt Polly were having a discussion early one Saturday morning.
Tom:	Aw, Aunt Polly, come on, don't make me stay home today. Me and some of the boys was fixin' to catch some frogs down by the creek.

Aunt Polly:	Tom, now I made myself quite clear. You are to stay within the confines of our home today. After all, don't you remember all of the ways you have gotten into trouble lately?
Group 1:	List and tell at least five ways Tom could have gotten into trouble in the past few days.
Tom:	But Aunt Polly, it just ain't fair that I have to stay at home today.
Aunt Polly:	I may be strict, Tom, but I am also quite fair. Why, you should be thankful that I am as lenient with you as I am. But don't forget to finish all of the jobs that I have assigned you.
Group 2:	List and tell ten jobs that Tom has been given by Aunt Polly.
Narrator:	Tom hadn't been working very long, when his cousin Sid came strolling around the back of the house.
Sid:	Hey, Tom, what are you doing?
Tom:	What's it look like I'm doing? I'm working at this rotten job that Aunt Polly gave me to do.
Sid:	That's too bad.
Tom:	Yeah, it is. Say, Sid, what would you think of taking a few of these jobs off my hands?
Sid:	No, I don't think so.
Tom:	I'll make it worth your while.
Sid:	How are you going to do that?
Tom:	Well, I'll tell you what I'll do . . .
Group 3:	List and tell five things Tom might offer Sid to do some of his jobs.
Sid:	Is that all? Sorry Tom, but I don't think that I want any of those things.
Tom:	Are you crazy Sid? Those were my best things in the whole world!
Sid:	You'll have to do better.
Tom:	How?
Sid:	Well, if you really want me to take over some of your jobs, then you'll have to . . .
Group 4:	List and tell five things that Sid really wants from Tom.
Tom:	Sid, I knew you was no good, but now I know you're just plum crazy. I ain't never gonna give you none of that stuff you just asked for.
Sid:	Suit yourself. And have a good time finishing all of your chores.
Narrator:	Tom continued working throughout the morning. Actually though, Tom didn't work so much as he . . .
Group 5:	List and tell six things Tom did instead of working.
Narrator:	Long about noon, Huck Finn happened to be walking by Tom's house. Huck stopped and shouted to Tom.
Huck:	Hey there Tom, what'cha doin?
Tom:	Aw, can't you see I'm killing myself with work?
Huck:	Too bad. I was hopin' you and me could take off and head out to the graveyard.
Tom:	What for Huck?
Huck:	Don't you remember? Tonight is one full week after a full moon on the first Saturday of summer.

Tom:	So?
Huck:	Tom, I can't believe you're being so lame-brained. A night like this happens only once every hundred years. And if you and me go out to the graveyard and wait till midnight . . .
Group 6:	Tell what will happen on this particular night.
Tom:	I would love to go with you Huck, but I got to stay here tonight cause of Aunt Polly.
Huck:	You leave that to me. What we need is a diversion so that you can slip away. Because we can't miss being out at the graveyard tonight, besides what I told you was going to happen, we might just get lucky and find where ol' Muff Potter buried his sack of gold ten years ago before he mysteriously disappeared,
Group 7:	Tell what diversion Huck creates so that he and Tom can escape.
Narrator:	Tom and Huck spent that day roaming through Hannibal, swimming in the river, playing marbles with their mates, and catching frogs in the creek. By the time midnight approached, Tom and Huck were in the graveyard.
Tom:	What time is it Huck?
Huck:	Near as I can tell, it's nigh on to midnight.
Tom:	Well, I ain't scared none, are you Huck?
Huck:	Me, scared? No, I ain't scared none. No sir, not me. Now all's we have to do is wait for the moonlight to cast a shadow from this here oak tree and that should point to the lost gold.
Tom:	Say Huck . . . hey, what's that comin' up over the hill yonder?
Huck:	Why it's Old Joe and Doc Marples.
Tom:	What are they doin'?
Huck:	It looks like they're digging up something. Yeah, they are. Tom, I can see them now. Look, Old Joe's dug up something all right. Can you make out what it is?
Huck:	It looks like a big sack. I'll bet it's Muff Potter's gold.
Tom:	Huck, we got to get that gold from them somehow.
Huck:	How we going to do that Tom? All's we got between us is nineteen marbles, a pocket knife, a ball of string, three frogs in a sack, a dead crow, a ripped sheet, six rocks and a candle.
Group 8:	Using any or all of these objects, tell how Tom and Huck can use them to get the gold away from Old Joe and Doc Marples.
Tom:	Huck, it worked! We did it. We got the gold!
Huck:	We sure did, Tom!
Tom:	We got the gold Huck! We got it! Hey, but what are we going to do with it?
Group 9:	Tell what Tom and Huck will do with the gold. Think of ten things. Remember the time is the late 1800s.
Narrator:	Tom and Huck head back to Tom's house where they are greeted by Aunt Polly. At first she is upset with Tom, but she begins to soften when Tom tells her . . .
Group 10:	Tell what Tom says to Aunt Polly.
Aunt Polly:	Well, Tom, you're quite a boy, and I guess I do love you. But come morning, I still might have a job or two for you to do.

WORKS CITED

Abbott, S. & Grose, C. (1998). "'I know English so many Mrs. Abbott': Reciprocal discoveries in a linguistically diverse classroom." *Language Arts,* 75, 175–184.

Adams, M. (1994). *Beginning to read.* Cambridge, MA: MIT Press.

Almasi, J. F. (2003). *Teaching strategic processes in reading.* New York: Guilford.

Anderson, R. C., Heibert, E. H., Scott, J. A., & Wilkinson, A. G. (1985). *Becoming a nation of readers: The report of the Commission on Reading.* Champaign-Urbana, IL: Center for the Study of Reading.

Apol, L. & Harris, J. (1999). "Joyful noises: Creating poems for voices and ears." *Language Arts,* 76, 314–321.

Armbruster, B. B., Lehr, F., & Osborn, J. (2001). *Put reading first: The research building blocks for teaching children to read.* Jessup, MD: National Institute for Literacy.

Au, K., Carroll, J. H., & Scheu, J. A. (2001). *Balanced literacy instruction.* Norwood, MA: Christopher Gordon.

Barton, B. & Booth, D. (1990). *Stories in the classroom: Storytelling, reading aloud and roleplaying with children.* Markham, Ontario: Pembroke.

Barrett-Pugh, C. & Rohl, M. (2001). "Learning in two languages: A bilingual program in Western Australia." *Reading Teacher,* 57, 664–676.

Berthoff, A. E. (1981). *The making of meaning: Metaphors, models, and maxims for writing teachers.* Portsmouth, NH: Boynton/Cook Heinemann.

Bishop, W. (1998). *Released into language.* Portland, ME: Calendar Islands Publishers.

Booth, D. (1994). *Story drama: Reading, writing and roleplaying across the curriculum.* Markham, Ontario: Pembroke.

Booth, D. & Moore, B. (1988). *Poems please! Sharing poetry with children.* Markham, Ontario: Pembroke.

Bruner, J. (1979). *On knowing: Essays for the left hand.* Cambridge, MA: Harvard University Press.

Buss, K. & Karnowski, L. (2000). *Reading and writing literacy genres.* Newark, DE: International Reading Association.

Collins, J. (1998). *Strategies for struggling writers.* New York: Guilford.

Coody, B. (1997). *Using literature with young children.* Madison, WI: Brown & Benchmark Publishers.

Cooper, P. J. & Collins, R. (1992). *Look what happened to frog.* Scottsdale, AZ: Gorsuch Scarisbrick.

Cope, B. & Kalantzis, M. (1993). "The power of literacy and the literacy of power." In Bill Cope and Mary Kalantzis (Eds.), *The power of literacy: A genre approach to teaching writing.* Pittsburgh: University of Pittsburgh Press.

Cramer, E. & Castle, M. (1994). "Developing lifelong readers." In E. Cramer and M. Castle (Eds.), *Fostering a love of reading* (pp. 1–10). Newark, DE: International Reading Association.

Csikszentmihalyi, M. (1991). "Literacy and intrinsic motivation." In Stephen R. Graubard (Ed.), *Literacy: An overview by 14 experts* (pp. 115–141). New York: Noonday.

Davis, E. J. (1997). "Bringing literature to life through Reader's Theatre." In Nicholas J. Karolides (Ed.), *Reader response in elementary classrooms* (pp. 113–136). Mahwah, NJ: Lawrence Erlbaum Associates.

de Bono, E. (1990). *Lateral thinking.* New York: Harper & Row.

Diamond, M. & Hopson, J. (1998). *Magic trees of the mind: How to nurture your child's intelligence, creativity, and healthy emotions from birth through adolescence.* New York: Dutton.

Dunn, M. (2001). "Aboriginal literacy: Reading the tracks." *Reading Teacher,* 54, 678–687.

Early, M. & Ericson, B. (1988). "The act of reading." In B. Nelms (Ed.), *Literature in the classroom: Readers, texts, and contexts* (pp. 31–44). Urbana: National Council of Teachers of English (NCTE).

Egan, K. (1997). *The educated mind.* Chicago: The University of Chicago Press.

———. (1992). *Imagination in teaching and learning.* Chicago: The University of Chicago Press.

Enciso, P. & Edmiston, B. (1997). "Drama and response to literature: Reading the story, re-reading 'the truth.'" In N. J. Karolides (Ed.), *Reader response in elementary classrooms.* Mahwah, NJ: Lawrence Erlbaum Associates.

Ferguson, P. M. & Young, T. A. (1996). "Literature talk: Dialogues, improvisation and patterned conversations with second language learners." *Language Arts,* 73, 597–600.

Fox, M. (1993). *Radical reflections.* New York: Harcourt Brace.

Fox, R. F. (1999). "Beating the moon: A reflection on media and literacy." *Language Arts,* 76, 479–482.

Furr, D. (2003). "Struggling readers get hooked on writing." *Reading Teacher,* 56, 518–525.

Gambell, T. J. (1993). "From experience to literary response: Actualizing readers through the response process." In S. Straw and D. Bogdan (Eds.), *Constructive reading: Teaching beyond communication* (pp. 30–45). Portsmouth, NH: Boynton/Cook Heinemann.

Gambrell, L. (Ed.). (1999). *Best practices in literacy instruction.* New York: Guilford.

Gardner, H. (1994). *The arts and human development.* New York: HarperCollins.

———. (1991). *The unschooled mind.* New York: HarperCollins.

Goodman, Y. & Goodman, K. (1994). "To err is human: Learning about language processes by analyzing miscues." In R. Ruddell, M. Ruddell, and H. Singers (Eds.), *Theoretical models and processes of reading.* Newark, DE: International Reading Association.

Gutiérrez, K., Baquedano-López, P., & Turner, M. G. (1997). "Putting language back into language arts: When the radical middle meet the third space." *Language Arts,* 74, 368–378.

Hadaway, N. L., Vardell, S. M., & Young, T. A. (2001). "Scaffolding oral language development through poetry for students learning English." *Reading Teacher,* 54, 796–806.

Hancock, M. R. (2000). *A celebration of literature and response.* New York: Merrill.

Harvey, S. & Goudvis, A. (2000). *Strategies that work: Teaching comprehension to ensure understanding.* York, ME: Stenhouse.

Havelock, E. (1991). "The oral-literate equation: A formula for the modern mind." In D. Olson and N. Torrance (Eds.), *Literacy and orality.* Cambridge: Cambridge University Press.

Healy, J. (1990). *Endangered minds.* New York: Simon & Schuster.

———. (1987). *Your child's growing mind.* New York: Doubleday.

Hillocks, Jr., G. (1995). *Teaching writing as reflective practice.* New York: Teachers College Press.

Huck, C., Hepler, S., Hickman, J., & Kiefer, B. (1997). *Children's literature in the elementary school.* Madison, WI: Brown & Benchmark.

Hunt, R. (1993). "Texts, tabloids, and utterances: Writing and reading for meaning, in and out of the classroom." In S. Straw and D. Bogdan (Eds.), *Constructive reading* (pp. 113–129). Portsmouth, NH: Boynton/Cook.

Iser, W. (1990). "Indeterminacy and the reader's response." In K. M. Newton (Ed.), *Twentieth-century literary theory.* New York: Macmillan.

Johns, J. & VanLeirsburg, P. (1994). "Promoting the reading habit." In E. Cramer and M. Castle (Eds.), *Fostering a love of reading* (pp. 91–103). Newark, DE: International Reading Association.

Karolides, N. J. (1997). "Reading process: Transactional theory in action." In N. J. Karolides (Ed.), *Reader response in elementary classrooms* (pp. 3–29). Mahwah, NJ: Lawrence Erlbaum Associates.

Kelso, E. B. (2000). "Talking to write: A mother and son at home." *Language Arts,* 77, 414–419.

Kern, D., Andre, W., Schilke, R., Barton, J., & McGuire, M. C. (2003). "Less is more: Preparing students for state writing assessments." *Reading Teacher,* 56, 816–826.

Kutz, E. & Roskelly, H. (1991). *An unquiet pedagogy: Transforming practice in the English classroom.* Portsmouth: NH: Boynton/Cook.

Langer, E. (1997). *The power of mindful learning.* Reading, MA: Addison-Wesley.

Langer, J. & Applebee, A. (1987). *How writing shapes thinking.* Urbana, IL: National Council of Teachers of English (NCTE).

Marc, D. (1995). *Bonfire of the humanities.* Syracuse, NY: Syracuse University Press.

Martens, P. (1997). "What miscue analysis reveals about word recognition and repeated reading: A view through the 'miscue window.'" *Language Arts,* 74, 600–609.

Martinez, M., Roser, N. L., & Strecker, S. (1999). " 'I never thought I could be a star': A Reader's Theatre ticket to fluency." *Reading Teacher,* 52, 326–334.

McCracken, R. & McCracken, M. (1998). *Stories, songs and poetry to teach reading and writing.* Winnipeg: Pegasus.

McKean, B. (2001). "Speak the speech, I pray you! Preparing to read aloud dramatically." *Reading Teacher,* 54, 358–360.

Meek, M. (1991). *On being literate.* Portsmouth, NH: Heinemann.

Moore, D., Temple, F., Juntunen, K., & Temple, C. (1989). *Classroom strategies that work.* Portsmouth, NH: Heinemann.

Moore, S. R. (1995). "Questions for research into reading-writing relationships and text structure knowledge." *Language Arts,* 72, 598–606.

Morado, C., Koenig, R., & Wilson, A. (1999). "Mini-performances, many stars! Playing with stories." *Reading Teacher,* 53, 116–123.

Murray, D. M. (1996). *Crafting a life: In essay, story, poem.* Portsmouth, NH: Boynton/Cook Publishers.

National Reading Panel. (2000). *Teaching children to read: An evidence-based assessment of the scientific research literature on reading and its implications for reading instruction* (National Institute of Health Pub. No. 00-4769). Washington, DC: National Institute of Child Health and Human Development.

Nell, V. (1994). "The insatiable appetite." In E. Cramer and M. Castle (Eds.), *Fostering a love of reading* (pp. 41–52). Newark, DE: International Reading Association.

Neuman, S. B. & Celano, D. (2001). "Books aloud: A campaign to 'put books in children's hands.'" *Reading Teacher,* 54, 550–557.

Noden, H. R. (1999). *Image grammar: Using grammatical structures to teach writing.* Portsmouth, NH: Boynton/Cook Heinemann.

Ong, W. (1982). *Orality and literacy.* New York: Routledge.

Orr, D. (2000). "Like, whatever . . . An epidemic of inarticulacy." *Utne Reader,* 100, 28–29.

Polette, K. (1998). "Igniting literacy: Enhancing critical reading with F.I.R.E." *The State of Reading: Journal of the Texas State Reading Association,* 4, 9–18.

Popp, M. (1996). *Teaching language and literature in elementary classrooms.* Mahwah, NJ: Lawrence Erlbaum Associates.

Postman, N. (1985). *Amusing ourselves to death.* New York: Penguin.

Pressley, M. (1998). *Reading instruction that works.* New York: Guilford.

Probst, R. E. (1988). "Readers and literary texts." In B. Nelms (Ed.), *Literature in the classroom: Readers, texts, and contexts* (pp. 19–29). Urbana: National Council of Teachers of English (NCTE).

Rasinski, T. V. (2000). "Speed does matter in reading." *Reading Teacher,* 54, 146–159.

Ratey, J. (2002). *A user's guide to the brain.* New York: Vintage.

Ray, K. W. (1999). *Wondrous words: Writers and writing in the elementary classroom.* Urbana: National Council of Teachers of English (NCTE).

Resnick, L. (1991). "Literacy in and out of school." In Stephen R. Graubard (Ed.), *Literacy: An overview by 14 experts* (pp. 15–32). New York: Noonday.

Richards, M. (2000). "Be a good detective: Solve the case of oral reading fluency." *Reading Teacher,* 53, 534–539.

Rothlein, L. & Meinbach, A. (1996). *Legacies: Using children's literature in the classroom.* New York: HarperCollins.

Rose, C. & Nichol, M. J. (1997). *Accelerated learning for the 21st century.* New York: Dell.

Rumelhart, D. (1994). "Toward an interactive model of reading." In M. R. Ruddel and H. Singer (Eds.), *Theoretical models and processes of reading* (4th ed., pp. 849–864). Newark, DE: International Reading Association.

Samuels, S. J. (2002). "Reading fluency: Its development and assessment." In A. E. Farstrup and S. J. Samuels (Eds.), *What research has to say about reading instruction* (pp. 166–183). Newark, DE: International Reading Association.

Sanders, B. (1995). *A is for ox: The collapse of literacy and the rise of violence in an electronic age.* New York: Vintage.

Scheuer, J. (1999). *The sound bite society: Television and the American mind.* New York: Four Walls Eight Windows.

Sinatra, R. (1994). "Literature and the visual arts." In E. Cramer and M. Castle (Eds.), *Fostering a love of reading* (pp. 104–117). Newark, DE: International Reading Association.

Singer, D. & Singer, J. (1990). *The house of make-believe: Children's play and the developing imagination.* Cambridge, MA: Harvard University Press.

Smith, F. (1997). *Reading without nonsense.* New York: Teachers College Press.

———. (1994). *Writing and the writer.* Hillsdale, NJ: Lawrence Erlbaum Associates.

Sorensen, M. & Lehan, B. (Eds.). (1995). *Teaching with children's books: Paths to literature-based instruction.* Urbana, IL: National Council of Teachers of English (NCTE).

Stewig, J. W. (1980). *Read to write.* New York: Richard C. Owen Publishers, Inc.

Stayter, F. Z. & Allington, R. (1991). "Fluency and the understanding of texts." *Theory into Practice,* 30, 143–148.

Temple, C. & Gillet, J. (1996). *Language and literacy.* New York: HarperCollins.

Tierney, R., John, R., & Dishner, E. (1995). *Reading strategies and practices: A compendium.* New York: Allyn & Bacon.

Ur, P. (1996). *A course in language teaching: Practice and theory.* Cambridge: Cambridge University Press.

Vukelich, C., Christie, J., & Enz, B. (2002). *Helping young children learn language and literacy.* Boston: Allyn & Bacon.

Vygotsky, L. S. (1978). *Mind in society.* Cambridge, MA: Harvard University Press.

———, (1962). *Thought and language.* Cambridge, MA: MIT Press.

Whyte, D. (1994). *The heart aroused.* New York: Doubleday.

Zecker, L. B. (1999). "Different texts, different emergent writing forms." *Language Arts,* 76, 483–490.

Ziegler, A. (1984). *The writing workshop,* Vol. 1. New York: Teachers & Writers Collaborative.

Zumthor, P. (1990). *Oral poetry.* Trans. by Katheryn Murphy-Judy. Minneapolis, MN: University of Minnesota Press.

INDEX